BUFFETT
STEP-BY-STEP

AN INVESTOR'S
WORKBOOK

FINANCIAL TIMES
MANAGEMENT

About our books

We work with leading authors to develop the
strongest ideas in business and finance, bringing
cutting-edge thinking and best practice to a
global market.

Under the Financial Times Pitman Publishing
imprint we craft high quality books which help
readers to understand and apply their content,
whether studying or at work.

To find out more please visit our website:
www.ftmanagement.com

BUFFETT
STEP-BY-STEP

AN INVESTOR'S
WORKBOOK

Learn to Analyze and
Apply the Techniques of the
Master Investor

RICHARD SIMMONS

FINANCIAL TIMES
PITMAN PUBLISHING

FINANCIAL TIMES
MANAGEMENT

LONDON · SAN FRANCISCO
KUALA LUMPUR · JOHANNESBURG

*Financial Times Management delivers the knowledge,
skills and understanding that enable students,
managers and organisations to achieve their ambitions,
whatever their needs, wherever they are.*

London Office:
128 Long Acre, London WC2E 9AN
Tel: +44 (0)171 447 2000
Fax: +44 (0)171 240 5771
Website: www.ftmanagement.com

A Division of Financial Times Professional Limited

First published in Great Britain 1999

ISBN 0 273 63028 8

British Library Cataloguing in Publication Data
A CIP catalogue record for this book can be obtained
from the British Library.

3 5 7 9 10 8 6 4

Typeset by M Rules
Printed and bound in Great Britain by
Redwood Books Ltd.

*The Publishers' policy is to use paper manufactured
from sustainable forests.*

ABOUT THE AUTHOR

Richard Simmons holds an MA from Oxford and an MBA from City University. He worked for twelve years in banking, setting up along the way two acquisition finance units. He is a non-executive director of one London quoted company, Optoplast Plc, and consultant to a number of others, specializing in strategy. He is currently establishing a new venture capital and fund management company and hopes to practise what he preaches. He is a successful private investor.

FOR REBECCA,
who gave me the reason to begin.

CONTENTS

Acknowledgments

I should like to acknowledge the help of the following people: Richard Stagg, a professional publisher; Heather, Justine, Anita, and Lilian, who held my hand throughout; Rebecca, Daniel, Melissa, Claire, Michael, and Paul, who have done it for real; my parents and Joanne, who knew when to help; and the directors of Henry Ansbacher & Co. Limited, who liberated me.

I have found *Forbes Greatest Business Stories Of All Time* by Daniel Gross (www.hoovers.com) and *Buffett* by Roger Lowenstein useful and well-written sources, and am happy to acknowledge them here. Warren Buffett recommends Chapters 8 and 20 of *The Intelligent Investor* by Ben Graham, and you will find further recommended reading in Chapter 3 of this book.

By far the most intelligent and creative writing on investment available is Warren Buffett's own. You will find his classic *Chairman's Letters* on the internet at www.berkshirehathaway.com. A two-volume bound set of the letters from 1977 to 1995 is available for $30 from:

Berkshire Hathaway Inc.,
3555 Farnam Street,
Suite 1440,
Omaha, NE 68131, USA.

PART 1

GETTING
STARTED

How to use this book

How the workbook is structured

This book has two aims: to identify the roots and justification of certain investment techniques, and to show how these techniques were developed and applied by the most successful investor of our time. By the time you complete the book, you should be able to apply the same methods to your own investment decisions.

The first part of the book tells the story of Berkshire Hathaway Inc. and its principal shareholder, Warren Buffett, emphasizing the business decisions he has made. An outline of the practices of the major investors and writers who shaped Buffett's thoughts follows. The second part analyzes the intellectual foundations of this investment method. Three key concepts are examined – *familiarity*, *intrinsic value*, and *margin of safety*. Along the way, the central tenets of modern corporate-finance theory are scrutinized and found wanting.

> By the time you complete the book, you should be able to apply the same methods to your own investment decisions.

The most important part of the book follows. Detailed case studies present the publicly available information as it was available to Buffett when he made his investments. These facts are analyzed and a business valuation is generated in each case using the techniques explained in the earlier parts of the book. 'What was actually paid' and 'What happened next' sections finish off each case. After each case a number of exercises test your ability to apply the lessons of the examples.

Using the case studies

Each case study exemplifies some or all of the techniques developed and explained in the earlier parts of the book. Most of the analysis is understandable in this context. Some of the more detailed explanations do require a basic familiarity with company accounts but most explanations are non-technical or start from basics. Full data for all of the case companies, a glossary, and a simple valuation model is included on a PC-readable 3.5 inch disk. Please send a check or postal order for £15/$27 to:

After each case a number of exercises test your ability to apply the lessons of the examples.

Richard Simmons
91 Odhams Walk
London WC2H 9SE
United Kingdom

Completing the exercises

At the end of every case there are some questions to test your ability to understand the data and analysis in the foregoing chapter. Suggested answers are at the end of the book and further questions are on the free disk. Bear in mind that there are no exact answers – the more subtle your understanding, the more complex your solution.

Applying the techniques

An even better way of making use of this book is to try to apply what you have learned to your actual or contemplated investments. In particular, you should be able to answer to your own satisfaction the following questions:

- *Do I understand why people buy this product from this company?*
- *Will this company be able to increase its prices and volumes in the long term?*
- *Is management able, honest, and good at allocating capital?*
- *What is the medium-term sustainable return to incremental equity?*

- *What is the value of the company?*
- *Is there an attractive margin between value and price?*

Remember: no one forces you to invest. If you cannot answer these questions, pass on the opportunity.

BACKGROUND

1

The Warren Buffett Story

Warren Edward Buffett was born in Omaha, Nebraska in August 1930. His father was a stockbroker and congressman, and the young Warren seems to have picked up an interest in stocks at his father's brokerage, together with a certain conservatism. Although he bought his first shares when aged 11, he was already a veteran businessman. On a family holiday in 1936 he broke up a six-pack of Cokes and sold the bottles individually at a profit. Coca-Cola of course features later on in this story (profit per six-pack – five cents, profit to date on the stock – $12 billion) but it is striking how often he has returned to the scenes of an earlier success: a mammoth delivery round of almost 500 newspapers a day in his teens centered on the *Washington Post* (he had made $5000 from this by the time he was 16), and American Express and Disney, which he bought and sold in the early 1960s, were early notable coups to which he returned more permanently in the 1990s.

> **Sometimes agreeing and sometimes disagreeing with Graham over individual securities, Buffett first emulated then superseded his master.**

After a short spell at the Wharton School in Pennsylvania, Buffett headed off to Columbia Business School and his manifest destiny – Benjamin Graham. Graham's decisive influence on the young Buffett is described in Chapter 3. Buffett spent a couple of years working at his father's brokerage before joining Graham's own mutual fund, Graham-Newman, on Wall Street. Sometimes agreeing and sometimes disagreeing with Graham over individual securities, Buffett first emulated then superseded his master. In the six years to 1956, he turned $10 000 into $140 000, far surpassing both Graham-Newman and the average stock market return. From the examples of stocks we know he bought in this period it seems that Buffett was essentially following Graham's lead. He was often buying at a discount to either net assets or net current assets, but would work harder to root out the necessary information in an age when corporate disclosure was often minimal. Graham himself retired in 1956, nominating only the 26-year-old Buffett as his intellectual successor. Graham-Newman was wound up and Buffett returned home to Omaha to start his own investment partnership.

BUFFETT PARTNERSHIP LTD

Buffett's reputation, his facility with numbers, his legendary memory, and self-confidence, soon attracted capital. Family, followers of Graham, neighbors, old college friends, and local professionals all put their faith in this young investor. There were one or two unusual conditions to the investment partnerships established at this time. First, investors committed their capital blind – only Buffett knew what was being bought and sold; second, the partners took their return first, typically 4 per cent p.a., before Buffett was paid anything. After this first 4 per cent, the remaining gain was split 75 per cent to the partners and 25 per cent to Buffett. A falling portfolio or one showing only modest growth would have netted Buffett nothing.

> **Buffett's reputation, his facility with numbers, his legendary memory, and self-confidence, soon attracted capital. Family, followers of Graham, neighbors, old college friends, and local professionals all put their faith in this young investor.**

In the first few years the partnership closely followed classic Graham techniques, buying assets at bargain prices.

CHARLIE MUNGER

Munger is Buffett's vice-chairman and partner at Berkshire Hathaway. He worked as a boy at Warren's grandfather's grocery store in Omaha, and I am sure that this link with his past appealed to Buffett. Munger, too, wanted to be rich and when they met as adults he had started his own law firm. Munger thought Buffett's "racket" was a surer path to wealth than the law and started his own investment partnership in 1962. For the eight years in which it is possible to make a comparison, Munger's partnership not only easily outpaced the indices, it even beat Buffett's partnership. The two men found that they had a lot in common and were increasingly treading on each other's toes as they considered similar investments. Over the 1970s they worked increasingly as a team and finally merged all of their common interests into Berkshire.

Munger has acted as Buffett's sounding-board for almost 40 years and they respect each other in a way that does not extend to many outsiders, but Munger is a quite different personality. By all reports astonishingly bright (like Buffett), he has also been more open to the world and, one gathers, freer with his wealth, particularly to charities (although Buffett is reckoned to be a generous and anonymous donor). It may be symbolic that Wesco, Berkshire's 80 per cent subsidiary, which Munger chairs, pays a dividend while Berkshire does not.

The most important shift Munger has initiated is Buffett's move from classic Graham investing. This is described in Chapter 3.

PSYCHOLOGY

Buffett has returned to his roots constantly in his career – from running his business in his hometown to his investments. In six of the seven case studies in Part 4 there is a personal and financial connection with the investee that goes back decades. He is conservative but he uses it to his advantage. He never invests sentimentally but uses the familiarity and knowledge that history brings to make investments when a price opportunity arises. His single most important trait as an investor is, therefore, his self-discipline: he does not pretend to understand what he cannot, such as technology stocks; he tries to understand as thoroughly as he is able those companies that are within his circle of competence, and he will not invest unless and until he is sure that the price available presents a safe discount to intrinsic value. Most investors fall down, as a matter of personality, in one of these three areas – by investing on a tip, for example, or by selling in a panic when prices drop. If you can bring yourself to see investing as a life-long activity, where each decision you take will have consequences over many years, you should be able to take your decisions more slowly and conscientiously. This does all beg a more important question.

WHAT'S MONEY FOR?

Although he is one of the richest men in the world, Buffett has a modest lifestyle. He lives in the house he bought 40 years ago and eats in the same restaurants. Because Berkshire has not paid a dividend for 30 years and Buffett has not sold any stock, and intends never to do so, 99 per cent of his wealth is in a form that he cannot spend (under Munger's influence, Berkshire distributes a small per centage of its earnings to charities). He lives off a modest salary and some private savings. When he dies, his family will receive a small inheritance, but the bulk will go to charitable trusts. The main aim, however, is to allow Berkshire to keep on running as it always has.

> He never invests sentimentally but uses the familiarity and knowledge that history brings to make investments when a price opportunity arises. His single most important trait as an investor is, therefore, his self-discipline: he does not pretend to understand what he cannot, such as technology stocks; he tries to understand as thoroughly as he is able those companies that are within his circle of competence, and he will not invest unless and until he is sure that the price available presents a safe discount to intrinsic value.

My own belief is that it was Buffett's ambition to become the wealthiest man in the world, and to do so from scratch. To his pleasure, this involved personal frugality and sticking to those things he knew best.

Most other people have other, and less materialistic, dreams. I would hope that you are able to use such wealth as investing brings you as a means to those dreams and not as an end.

2

The Berkshire Hathaway Story

CORPORATE HISTORY

Although Berkshire Hathaway is now one of the most valuable enterprises in the world, its roots lie in the nineteenth-century world of Massachusetts cotton mills. The Berkshire and Hathaway firms had traded on into the twentieth century but, facing intense competition, merged in 1955. Anticipated cost savings were not enough to restore profitability, however, and the combination chalked up losses of $10.1 million on sales of $530 million from 1955 until 1964. At this stage its balance sheet was as follows:

$ Millions			
Cash	0.9	Debt	2.5
Receivables and inventories	19.1	Payables	3.2
Property, plant, and equipment	7.8	Equity	22.1

There were 1.1 million shares outstanding to give a book value per share of $19.

The Buffett Partnership started buying stock at $8 in 1962, a clear example of the Graham discipline; current assets minus all liabilities equaled c.$13 per share giving a margin of safety of 38 per cent (you will learn these calculations in Chapter 11). As Buffett bought more he seems to have become enamored with the company. Ending up with

49 per cent of the stock, in 1965 he was elected a director. The average cost of this stake was reported as $15 per share, a premium to Graham's "net working capital" guideline, but still a respectable 21 per cent discount to book. What most seems to have attracted Buffett was the prospect of squeezing investment and shrinking current assets with the consequent generated cash being diverted into more profitable areas. As it happened, 1965 and 1966 were two rare good years for the textile business, but almost every proposal for reinvestment made by operating management was vetoed by their new director. As cash was produced from profits or liquidating working assets, Buffett considered investment ideas.

> **What most seems to have attracted Buffett was the prospect of squeezing investment and shrinking current assets with the consequent generated cash being diverted into more profitable areas.**

The first and, in some ways, most important acquisition was an insurance company. The GEICO case covers insurance in more detail, but it is worth considering here why Buffett has been so attracted to this industry. Most insurers make money in two ways. First, in return for insuring against defined risks they take a fee or premium from customers. Take away the actual payments made for valid claims and overheads and you have the underwriting profit. Many insurers actually make an underwriting loss and rely on the second source of profits: in the time between taking premiums and paying out for claims, the company invests the cash and takes the profit. Berkshire Hathaway's insurance subsidiaries exploit this situation in three ways:

1 They work hard to make an underwriting profit. This first acquisition, National Indemnity Co., specialized in unusual risks. Similarly, one of Berkshire's biggest lines of business today is catastrophic reinsurance risk, that is, it provides cover to smaller insurance companies in the earthquake/hurricane, etc. field which want to pass on excess risk. Berkshire's ability to price such risk accurately, its willingness to be selective (it will only insure if it thinks it will produce an underwriting profit) and, these days, its vast size and, therefore, almost unrivaled ability to take on large

policies, all help it achieve profitability. In the GEICO business, which provides more routine automobile cover, it strives to be the lowest-cost insurer in the field, meaning it can compete on price and still turn a profit.

2 In many of the fields in which Berkshire specializes there is a long gap between underwriting a policy and payout. Relative to the size of its revenue from issuing policies, Berkshire has an unusually high float. "Float" is essentially the money the insurer holds and can invest for its own benefit but one day expects to pay out. Berkshire's float in its new insurance business was $17 million in 1967. Several acquisitions, significant organic growth and 30 years later, it was $7.5 billion.

3 Because its insurance companies generally make an underwriting profit, Berkshire's float is effectively an interest-free loan from the policyholders. The most significant effect of the insurance activities on its results has been the spectacular return achieved from the invested float. When people think of Berkshire, they think of its wonderful investments –

> "Float" is essentially the money the insurer holds and can invest for its own benefit but one day expects to pay out.

Gillette, Coca-Cola, Disney. These would not exist if the capital to invest had not been provided by the insurance businesses.

Berkshire paid $8.6 million for National Indemnity. Since Berkshire has not paid a dividend since 1967 retained profits have been another important source of capital. Using these generated profits and the float a number of other purchases of entire businesses were made, notably the Illinois National Bank & Trust, and Sun Newspapers of Omaha.

In 1970, the Buffett Partnership was wound up and partners were given the option of shares in Berkshire Hathaway and another investment, Diversified Retailing, or cash. Buffett decided to stick with Berkshire and ended up with 29 per cent and the chairmanship. After the 1973–4 market crash Buffett picked up more stock, reportedly in the $40s, at a time when Berkshire's per share book value was in the $70s, a discount of c.40 per cent.

Director's shareholdings in Berkshire Hathaway, 1997

Name	Number of shares	Voting power (%)
Warren Buffett	478 232	39.7
Susan Buffett	37 007	3.1
Malcolm Chace	14 239	1.1
Charles Munger	18 790	1.6

Note: Susan Buffett is Warren Buffett's wife; his and her totals may include double-count. Malcolm Chace is part of the family who originally controlled Berkshire Hathaway.

The cash that Berkshire has generated from operations and insurance float has principally been invested in three ways:

Common stock investments

Through the stock market (with few exceptions, the New York Stock Exchange) significant minority stakes in large companies have been built up. Although a number have come and gone, notably some advertising agencies and publishers, many of the shareholdings first established in the 1970s and 1980s remain to this day.

Stock	Year first acquired	Cost $m	Market value $m, December 1997
American Express	1991	1393	4414
Coca-Cola	1988	1299	13 338
Walt Disney	1977	381	2135
Freddie Mac	1988	329	2683
Gillette	1989	600	4821
Washington Post	1973	11	841
Wells Fargo	1989	413	2271

Each of the above is covered by a case study, except Freddie Mac, whose ground is efficiently covered in the Wells Fargo and American Express cases. The Washington Post Company stake was bought at the low point of the 1973–4 crash. Buffett has always loved media companies, the best of them functioning as gatekeepers to a group of readers; if you were an advertiser and wanted to reach a reader in a town where the *Washington Post* published the main newspaper, you had little choice but to pay up. Walt Disney, although best known for its animated films and theme parks, became a Berkshire investment when it merged with Capital Cities/ABC, a television production and broadcasting group. Known for its outstanding management, Capital Cities was another group owning near-monopoly outlets irresistible to advertisers, this time television stations and a national broadcast network. Like the *Washington Post*, Wells Fargo was bought at a time when the stock market put a very low value on its earnings. Although Buffett has no particular love for banks Wells Fargo has superior economics to its competitors based on its low costs and, like the *Washington Post*, was available at a knock-down price. GEICO, now wholly-owned, is a similar story. American Express, another financial-services company, is dominant in certain fields with substantial barriers to entry. Finally, two consumer-goods companies, Coca-Cola and Gillette, are the leading brands in each of their markets with considerable international growth potential.

General Re merger

Berkshire has recently agreed to merge with General Re. This is by far the largest purchase the company has made, entailing the issuance of 277 200 new Berkshire shares, an increase of 22 per cent. Perhaps predictably, General Re is a reinsurer, a business Berkshire knows backwards. It was established in 1921 and now writes a hefty $6.5 billion in premiums per year from 61 offices around the world. It routinely enjoys a combined ratio of around 100 so we might value it at the sum of its cash, investments, debts and preference stock – c.$24.5 billion. Since Berkshire is issuing 277 200 new shares in exchange for this value, and Buffett is adamant that he will not give away more than he receives in a merger, we might conclude that he does not currently believe that Berkshire is worth more than $88 400 per share. Furthermore, if Berkshire is actually currently worth c.$46 000 (see below) existing Berkshire shareholders are getting a very good deal.

Wholly-owned companies

In addition to buying small stakes in quoted companies, Berkshire buys 90–100 per cent of some businesses. Usually this has been from founding family shareholders; in two cases, GEICO and FlightSafety, the companies were partially quoted and a public offer was made. Aside from these two a large number of smaller private businesses have been acquired. Although not as significant as the insurance business, the wholly-owned companies are meaningful contributors, declaring together $252 million net income in 1997.

Liquidity

When not buying minority or majority equity stakes Berkshire Hathaway, like other investors, holds cash and bonds to mop up surplus liquidity. It also borrows from time to time *particularly when it does not need to*. In this way it secures the finest terms and knows it has sufficient capital if an unmissable opportunity arises. However, total indebtedness is rarely high. Buffett has an aversion to debt and does not believe the extra returns it brings are worth the additional risk. In the late 1980s Berkshire decided to invest in a pool of convertible preferred stocks. A lot of publicity arose from the Salomon and USAir securities. More pertinently Buffett showed how his margin-of-safety doctrine could be applied to any sort of security, not just equities. The Gillette case demonstrates his logic in these cases.

When not buying minority or majority equity stakes Berkshire Hathaway, like other investors, holds cash and bonds to mop up surplus liquidity. It also borrows from time to time *particularly when it does not need to*. In this way it secures the finest terms and knows it has sufficient capital if an unmissable opportunity arises.

Berkshire has also periodically committed small amounts of capital to sectors with a racier reputation, such as arbitrage, silver, and oil derivatives. While this book does not detail these decisions, we know that Buffett used the same process to determine the attractiveness and price of these investments, chiefly the margin of safety.

THE MAGIC OF LEVERAGE

We have already looked at the considerable advantage that the insurance float has offered Berkshire. An equally important source of capital has been deferred taxation. Buffett has sensibly taken the view that what matters to an investor is his or her after-tax return. Happily, Buffett's preferred mode of investing for the long-term minimizes the tax cost to the business. As an example, let us compare two investors with $100. Investor A buys and holds shares in a company that does not pay a dividend and whose stock price moves up 10 per cent p.a. At the end of 20 years, A pays capital gains tax of, say, 35 per cent on selling the shares. His remaining cash is $1099. Investor B has $100 and buys and sells each year a different stock which appreciates 10 per cent. Even ignoring brokerage costs, which would in fact be significant, B has to pay 35 per cent of the

> **Buffett's preferred mode of investing for the long-term minimizes the tax cost to the business.**

gain each year and after 20 years has only $643. A's annual rate of return is 12.7 per cent, B's is 9.8 per cent. The difference is even more substantial if you are achieving the sort of annual capital growth Berkshire is enjoying. As with the float generated from insurance, Berkshire receives an interest-free loan, this time from the government, by agreeing to defer certain taxes; in 1997 these totaled $10.4 billion. So long as the business carries on in its current form, it can invest the money it owes in taxes and float for its own profit.

Another way of considering this is to ask what the effect would be if Berkshire had the benefit of neither float nor deferred tax. Equity funds of $23.4 billion in 1996, for example, would have to be supplemented by some $14.3 billion to support the same asset base, giving shareholders' funds of $36.9 billion. Berkshire has grown its book value per share 23.8 per cent p.a. on average over the last 32 years. The total asset base of $43.4 billion in 1996 would have had to grow by $5.6 billion in 1997, other things being equal, to provide a 23.8 per cent advance on $23.4 billion equity. But the same asset growth on equity of $36.9 billion is only 14.9 per cent:

1 (i) Berkshire in 1996 ($bn)

		Float and deferred taxes	14.3
		Other liabilities	5.7
Total assets	43.4	Equity	23.4

1 (ii) Projected one year

		Float and deferred taxes	14.3
		Other liabilities	5.7
Total assets	49.0	Equity	29.0
Asset growth = 12.9%		Equity growth = 23.8%	

2 (i) Berkshire without float or deferred taxes

		Float and deferred taxes	0
		Other liabilities	5.7
Total assets	43.4	Equity	37.7

2 (ii) Projected one year

		Float and deferred taxes	0
		Other liabilities	5.7
Total assets	49.0	Equity	43.3
Asset growth = 12.9%		Equity growth = 14.9%	

So there have been three elements to the growth in Berkshire's value. First and most importantly, the insurance business and the wholly-owned concerns have been acquired, in part, because they throw off cash – they are the perpetual motion machines of capitalism. Second, this cash has been well invested over long periods of time in the stock market, in wholly-owned operations and in other securities. These two effects together have driven up the book value of Berkshire. Finally, the stock market itself has rewarded this inexorable rise by marking Berkshire's value up at a considerable premium to book. Consequently, since 1962 the share price has risen at a compounded rate of 28.7 per cent taking Buffett's stake to a value of $34 billion. But without the magic of leverage the book value and share price might only have grown at 15 per cent p.a. taking this stake to a more modest value of $635 million – and very likely no one would ever have heard of Warren Buffett.

WHAT'S IT WORTH?

While the growth in Berkshire's book value has been impressive, and even more so when you consider that the number of shares in issue has only grown 8 per cent since 1965, it had, until the General Re merger, been outstripped by its market value. As we noted earlier, the stock went to a discount to book after the 1973–4 crash. Climbing steadily it started to trade at a premium consistently after 1983. At c.$70 000 per share in early 1998, it is at a 175 per cent premium to book value. In Chapter 11 we will consider the central topic of estimating intrinsic value. Berkshire's own intrinsic value is more difficult to judge than most companies' because

> While the growth in Berkshire's book value has been impressive, and even more so when you consider that the number of shares in issue has only grown 8 per cent since 1965, it has been outstripped by its market value.

periodic and unpredictable capital gains make up a large part of its earnings. However, here is a simple way to think about it. In 1997 the company made $627m after tax from its wholly-owned businesses, including $298m underwriting profit. If these businesses were sold or quoted in their own right they might be worth $12 billion, give or take. The investment assets of the rest of the group minus debt equalled $45 billion; together summing to $57 billion. If one tentatively accepts that the long-term liabilities, float and deferred taxes, are effectively free (so long as the business at least stays static, they do not need to be paid and eventually will be inflated away) this works out at $46 000 per share intrinsic value. Of course, since Messrs Graham, Munger, and Buffett teach above all else that one should only invest at a healthy discount to intrinsic value, this makes Berkshire Hathaway an unattractive stock for fresh investment at current prices.

3

Intellectual Antecedents and Influences

Buffett once said that his method was 85 per cent Graham and 15 per cent Fisher. We will see that this typically modest self-assessment ignores his own central contributions, but Graham and Fisher, as well as the other thinkers considered in this chapter, provide the intellectual underpinnings to Buffett's achievement.

BEN GRAHAM – PAYING 50 CENTS FOR A DOLLAR

Buffett's father was in the stock business himself and they appear to have been close but there is no doubt that Ben Graham was the most influential person in the young investor's intellectual development.

Graham was born in London in 1894, but was brought up in New York. There are some parallels with Buffett – a precocious intelligence, a natural money manager and a talented teacher. Graham, however, led the way. He went to work on Wall Street before the First World War, when the stock market was in its infancy, there being few issues other than railroads and other utilities. Bonds dominated the markets and common stocks were considered too speculative for many portfolios. Little public information was provided by the publicly traded corporations, but Graham had a talent for digging up data, particularly from the little-studied submissions to regulatory bodies. He pioneered what we now call security analysis, paying most attention to the balance sheet. A typical play would be a utility making modest profits and declaring little or no dividends but owning a valuable portfolio of cash and securities. Because of the low yield and lack of information the share price often traded at a drastic discount to the portfolio value. Graham saw his role as being twofold. First, through diligent research he identified these companies and assigned an *intrinsic value* to the enterprise. He bought stock at a discount to this value, employing a *margin of safety*. Second, he either waited for the market to recognize the intrinsic value or he took direct action to persuade company management to increase shareholder value, for example, by selling the hoarded portfolio or increasing the dividend. When the stock price rose to or above its intrinsic value, he sold out.

By 1923 Graham's reputation was such that friends, acquaintances and relatives were offering him money to invest. With a partner he established the Graham-Newman Corporation and, in various forms, this investment partnership was his livelihood until his retirement in 1956. He experienced the Crash of 1929 and subsequent depression and was able to see the market in all of its moods. Graham-Newman invested in straightforward undervalued situations as described above, but also in arbitrage, Chapter 8 (bankrupt) stocks, hedges, and other special situations. Graham's speciality became looking for companies trading for less than their net working capital – current assets (cash and other securities plus stock and receivables) minus all liabilities.

> Little public information was provided by the publicly traded corporations, but Graham had a talent for digging up data, particularly from the little-studied submissions to regulatory bodies. He pioneered what we now call security analysis, paying most attention to the balance sheet.

Graham's enduring reputation, however, is as a teacher. Having pioneered security analysis, he was famously generous in teaching others. He lectured for many years at Columbia (Buffett enrolled there purely to learn from Graham) and co-wrote two classic investment texts: *Security Analysis* and *The Intelligent Investor*. In his early years, and understandably while he was an employee of Graham's, Buffett was a slavish adherent of his teacher's mathematical methods – securities either passed the net working capital and other tests or they did not. Later he went his own way, but Buffett has always remained true to the core of Graham's insights.

Ben Graham's core concepts

Intrinsic value and margin of safety

The job of the investor is to estimate the true or objective value of a security and only pay a price that is substantially less. From this simple statement several rules follow:

- Only invest where there is enough information to make a reasonable estimate of intrinsic value.
- Only invest when there is a margin of safety.
- Only invest if you are prepared to wait for the market to recognize intrinsic value.

Successful investing is a good deal to do with intelligent appraisal combined with patience.

Market fluctuations

Graham distinguishes between speculators and investors. Speculators try to predict short-term price movements and buy and sell accordingly. Today this category includes technical analysts (who rely only on charts of historical price information), momentum investors (who buy on the principle that what goes up must continue to go up) and hedge fund managers (who try to second-guess the market). Investors buy on fundamental beliefs about the value of the underlying business and hold until that value is realized.

Graham believed that investors of his type had strong advantages over speculators. In a famous "parable" in *The Intelligent Investor* he introduces us to Mr Market. Mr Market is your partner in business. Every day he quotes a price at which he is prepared to buy your share in the business or at which you may buy his share. But he is something of a manic-depressive. On some days he is elated and values the share well above its true worth, and sometimes he is convinced the business is ruined and places a price on the business well below its true value. Do these different prices affect the intrinsic value of your business? No. Similarly, in the stock market the fluctuation of prices in itself gives us no information about the value of businesses in which we invest. It is true that on occasion some other investors possess relevant information we do not. In the majority of cases, though, the price movements only represent the volatile sentiments of Mr Market. Graham in fact sees Mr Market as our friend because these irrational price movements give us regular opportunities to buy below intrinsic value and sell above it. And if we employ a sufficient margin of safety between price and value, we can afford to wait for an appreciative market (or Mr Market) to come knocking.

> **Mr Market is your partner in business. Every day he quotes a price at which he is prepared to buy your share in the business or at which you may buy his share.**

PHILIP FISHER – THE BUSINESSLIKE APPROACH

If Graham solved a basic problem in finance – how to invest sensibly – he only did so by raising an equally large question: how do you estimate intrinsic value? It is no diminution of his achievement to point out that things were easier then. Because for much of the first half of this century stocks were out of fashion, it was not unusual to find companies trading well below the value of their net working capital. These were often what Buffett calls "cigar butts", previously favored companies that had hit hard times and were probably loss-making. Berkshire Hathaway was originally one of these. Partly through the example and teaching of Graham and his followers, these opportunities dried up.

> **Because for much of the first half of this century stocks were out of fashion, it was not unusual to find companies trading well below the value of their net working capital. These were often what Buffett calls "cigar butts", previously favored companies that had hit hard times and were probably loss-making.**

Philip Fisher found value in a different direction altogether. First as a security analyst for a San Francisco bank in 1928, and since

1931 running his own investment firm in California, he has concentrated on buying and holding the stock of companies likely to grow in the long term; he owned Motorola as his largest personal holding for over 20 years, for example. What sounds like common sense to anyone buying a business privately he applied to the public markets. Many of the principles he practiced are identical to Buffett's. In Chapter 5 we will look in more detail at how to use "scuttlebutt" or company information. Here are some other key pointers from Fisher.

Philip Fisher's core concepts

The job of the investor is to forecast industries and companies likely to grow in the long run and invest accordingly. The following rules follow:

- **Only invest in an industry you understand well.**

- **Research the company under consideration, its competitors, suppliers, and customers thoroughly, preferably face-to-face.**

- **Look for superiority in management.**

Fisher wrote lucidly about these principles in a number of books, notably *Common Stocks and Uncommon Profits* and *Developing an Investment Philosophy*. His greatest contribution is focusing investors on fundamentals. In passing he strongly disagreed with over-diversification and efficient markets theory, subjects which we will turn to shortly.

Fisher and Buffett part company in two respects. Fisher was fascinated by companies on the leading edge of technology. He (rightly) saw fantastic investment potential in industries transformed by aggressive research and development, such as electronics, chemicals, and machinery. Buffett has stayed away from these types of ventures – not only because they are outside his field of competence, but because they often provide a low return on capital invested. More fundamentally, Fisher says little about price. While he is concerned about overpaying he seems to believe that true growth companies deserve a premium. This is a long way from classic Graham.

INTRINSIC VALUE REVISITED

Under the influence of Charlie Munger, Buffett synthesized Graham and Fisher's concepts of intrinsic value. Buffett defined the intrinsic value of any investment as the discounted present value of its future cash flow. This ties in both Graham-type "cigar butts", where the cash realizable is a function of the liquidated value of its assets minus all its liabilities, and Fisher-type growth stocks where cash will be produced by future profits. Buffett and Munger realized that the latter are less certain. They mitigated the risk in two important ways. Crucially, they continued to apply a margin of safety: it may be more difficult to assess the future cashflows of Coca-Cola than its liquidated balance sheet value but you will be still be safe if you buy well below your estimate. Also, management of investee companies needed to be honest as well as competent, able to maximize future cashflows *and* direct surplus cash into profitable investment or back to the shareholders.

MICHAEL PORTER – A PARALLEL APPROACH

We shall see that Buffett has often sought to invest in businesses possessing economic franchises. His positive experiences with See's Candies and various newspaper groups may account for this. Certainly, he has shown little interest in the work of academic economists on this or any other topic. He is contemptuous of attempts to forecast interest-rate cycles, the general level of the stock market or the many other macroeconomic variables that distract today's analysts. Conversely, he is fascinated by the microeconomic. Although he usually does not interfere with management, he is formidably well informed about what we might call "key value drivers" and his annual reports are filled with detail of the *Buffalo News'* newshole (per centage of total space dedicated to news) or Nebraska Furniture Mart's sales per square foot.

At the more strategic level, his preferred companies have often displayed characteristics identified by Michael Porter as being associated with long-term success. Porter is a professor at the Harvard Business

School and is famous for a series of books that address this topic with rigor and common sense (unusual bedfellows in economics). In *Competitive Strategy*, in particular, he provides an analytical framework for analyzing industries and competitors. He suggests that five forces drive competition in an industry:

- the threat of new entrants
- the relative strength of customers
- the ability to substitute other products
- the relative strength of suppliers
- the degree of rivalry among existing competitors.

Buffett has often been attracted to companies that score well under this analysis. Newspapers that dominate a town's readership, for example, deter new entrants (the town will not support two papers), are in a good position to bargain with readers (by increasing the cover price and advertising rates), have no direct substitutes (this is less true as local television and national newspapers have developed in the USA), are well able to bargain with suppliers (paper supply and deliverers are commodities) and have no other local newspapers with which to compete. I would say that the first of these factors, barriers to entry, is what has most exercised Buffett's mind – many of his largest investments have dominated their industries in a way that has discouraged new entrants or condemned them to marginal profitability.

> The first of these factors, barriers to entry, is what has most exercised Buffett's mind – many of his largest investments have dominated their industries in a way that has discouraged new entrants or condemned them to marginal profitability.

Porter also writes about three strategies firms can adopt in order to outcompete their rivals:

- overall cost leadership
- differentiation
- focus.

GEICO, Berkshire Hathaway's principal insurance business, has had cost leadership in its industry for years. Gillette is differentiated from its competitors through its dominant brands and new product development. Nebraska Furniture Mart is ruthlessly focused on selling certain products in a certain geographical area as best it can. The truth is, though, that most Berkshire investments have something of all three factors about them. Whether it is a dominant brand name or the lowest possible costs, almost all businesses associated with Warren Buffett do not tempt competition.

OTHER INVESTMENT STYLES – CONTRASTING PHILOSOPHIES

It is worth running through some other investment methods and giving Buffett's objections.

Traders and mutual funds

Chartists, speculators, and hedge fund managers probably come at the bottom of the heap as far as Buffett is concerned. He would consider them gamblers rather than investors. Surprisingly, this crowd has had support from academic theorists in the last three decades. Efficient-market theorists, who have dominated business school theory until recently, believe all information about a company and its prospects is already in the market price. Therefore, unless one has inside information one cannot beat the market. This has encouraged investors either to look for "hidden" patterns in price histories or to be content with matching the market by diversifying portfolios as widely as possible. Buffett has no great argument with the latter approach for the casual investor and has indeed recently endorsed the ownership of index funds. But for the intelligent investor he insists that application of his principles, above all the margin of safety and being comfortable with the basic economics of the company, will enable long-term market outperformance.

Capital markets theory and EVA

Academics and security analysts keen to put investment theory on a scientific footing have developed a body of work and data that relies on identification of different types of risk. The argument is that investors suffer market risk and individual company risk and should be aware of the quantum in each case. Individual company risk is derived from the historic volatility of the company's stock price compared to market movements. Using these measures and a company's indebtedness one can measure its true cost of capital. For example, the higher a particular stock's relative volatility the riskier it is and, therefore, the higher the discount an investor will require before holding it. In reality, historic share price volatility tells us little about a company. Embracing the margin-of-safety principle, we should welcome volatility since it gives us more opportunity to invest at low prices. Remember Mr Market!

Consulting firms such as Stern Stewart and McKinsey have developed economic value added (EVA) and economic profit models that try to adapt cost of capital theories to more realistic investment practice. As we will see in Part 3, Buffett pays close attention to return on equity. He is much less interested in developing a precise measure of capital cost. Indeed, EVA's final rationale is MVA (market value added), an adjusted measure of stock appreciation, whereas Buffett-type investors want to appraise a company's intrinsic value quite separately from its price or price history.

> In reality, historic share price volatility tells us little about a company. Embracing the margin-of-safety principle, we should welcome volatility since it gives us more opportunity to invest at low prices.

THE PHASES OF BUFFETT

We have seen that Buffett started by finding value in discounted balance sheets. This became difficult as other investors imitated the method and as all investors became used to the idea that companies should trade at a premium to book value. Looking around for other ideas Buffett and Munger realized that future cashflow was, for some companies, a more enduring source of value than the price of their assets in a bankruptcy court.

Important themes from this chapter pervade Buffett's career. Whether you are investing in a stock, a bond, or buying a whole business, you must have a clear idea of its true worth or intrinsic value. Intrinsic value is a function of the cash that will be thrown off by the investment over its lifetime, discounted to its present value. That cash value may be as low as the book value of its net assets (sometimes it is not even that) or it may be dramatically higher for a business with good prospects; your job is to estimate it. But just as important is to have the discipline to pay a price that reflects a safe discount to this value. Over time the market will probably reflect that value. Even if it does not the weight of generated cash you receive should far exceed the price you paid.

> Intrinsic value is a function of the cash that will be thrown off by the investment over its lifetime, discounted to its present value.

Estimating future cashflows is in fact far from easy. We next consider how in practice to assess *intrinsic value* and *what to pay*.

PART 3

HOW TO INVEST

4

Being Value Aware –
The Three Value Questions

Before we can calculate intrinsic value we must have some idea of what future cashflow will be. For businesses, a logical starting place, likely to be the main source of cash, is profits. (We will see later that some profits are better than others.) Why do some companies make more money than others over time, even within the same industry?

It is easy to start a business. Savings, loans, and trade credit will be enough for most small businesses. Even large businesses with established market positions will attract competition from well-financed start-ups or companies looking to diversify. Nevertheless, some companies are able to grow profitability and return high rewards to shareholders over decades. Using the insights of Warren Buffett, sometimes with the help of Michael Porter, we can see how. Think again about the book value of a business – its plant, working capital, and liquidity. American Express has a book value of $8.5 billion and generates profit of $1.9 billion. Why can't General Electric or a big bank come along, make the same investment and take this profit for themselves? After all this is a 22.4 per cent return on investment, over three times as much as if the money was invested in treasuries tax-free. Of course, American Express already has competitors, but it cannot match this return. This is because American Express is adding value in ways that are difficult for its competitors and potential competitors to emulate. What makes this entrenchment possible? If you are looking for companies that will maximize profits over time, you must be able to answer the following three value questions.

THE THREE VALUE QUESTIONS

1. Does the company add value to its customers?

A company's profit is the difference between the cost of its inputs, including capital, and what it can sell the generated product or service for. Therefore, it is likely to maximize its profits over the long run if it can regularly produce at lower costs or sell at higher prices than its actual or potential competitors. In practice, sustaining lower costs is very difficult. For every store prepared to discount 50 per cent, there will be one quoting 60 per cent. If you establish a factory in Mexico, your rival will build one in Peru. A few businesses can establish long-run cost leadership, but most industries do not have one cost leader over time.

> A company's profit is the difference between the cost of its inputs, including capital, and what it can sell the generated product or service for. Therefore, it is likely to maximize its profits over the long run if it can regularly produce at lower costs or sell at higher prices than its actual or potential competitors.

A more enduring way for a company to enjoy growing profits is to deliver something the customer values and which is difficult to obtain elsewhere. These are different but related concepts. On a sunny day people will value ice cream highly and may be prepared to pay a price far in excess of its cost. But the presence of competition (many existing ice-cream vans and shops) and the threat of future competition (if prices were high others would buy vans) keep prices down. In many industries a good is desirable, but no one will pay a premium price. We might, therefore, look at what Porter has to say about both the producer–buyer relationship and disincentives to potential competitors.

Porter on customers

Businesses are likely to have power over their customers where any or all of the following are present:

- there are few threats from substitutes
- no one customer dominates turnover
- the business only supplies a small proportion of the customer's total purchases

- the product is differentiated from competitors' products
- it is costly for the customer to switch suppliers.

Many of Buffett's current largest investments readily fit the above. Gillette and Coca-Cola are mass-market consumer companies that, by definition, produce product that accounts for a fraction of their customers' total purchases. By and large (ignoring the wholesaler), their customers are small and do not combine to negotiate prices, and their products are readily differentiated both from competitors (Pepsi) and substitutes (water/orange juice).

Porter on barriers to entry

So the company has a product which is attractive to customers and for which they are prepared to pay a premium price. What stops new entrants competing away the price differential?

- If there are significant economies of scale in an industry, it may be costly and, therefore, risky for a competitor to reach an existing producer's cost structure.
- An established brand and customer loyalties take time and money to build up.
- Businesses that require substantial initial capital investment, such as large-scale car manufacturing, will deter those which would have to raise capital and pay a risk premium.
- There may be costs in switching products. These may be actual (retailers stocking a new ice-cream brand may need new freezers) or psychological (it is difficult to persuade people to try a new ice cream if they are happy with the existing product).
- Existing distributors may be so tied up by the existing product that new distribution channels have to be created.
- Expertise, patents, or exclusive supply agreements are difficult to break/replicate.
- Government may regulate or license entry (as it does in many broadcast media).

One might conclude that the ideal business is a monopoly, such as a utility or bridge, but in practice most such entities are heavily regulated by government so that they are non-profit making or have their pricing power severely curtailed.

Industry conditions

It is possible to make money in a declining industry – tobacco companies have increased their profits for years in face of falling demand (loyalty/addiction is so strong that they can increase prices to compensate). It is far easier however to maximize profits in a growing industry. Fisher differentiates between managements that are fortunate and able, and managements that are fortunate *because* they are able. In the former case they are fortunate if their industry is growing, relatively non-competitive, and has strong barriers to entry; in the latter case they must rely on their wits alone. Consideration of management leads us to the second value question.

2. Does management provide value to the company?

There are really two questions to ask yourself about management of a potential investment – are they competent and are they honest?

> Is management making efforts to maintain or attain cost leadership? Managers who let costs grow and then indulge in bouts of rationalizing with associated "exceptional" costs are seldom as able as those who routinely design processes to keep costs as low as possible.

Competence is of course a lodestone for any business. In this case we are looking for evidence that the company has obtained sustainable long-term advantages over its competitors and that these have been enhanced by current management. The factors that differentiate one company profitably from another which we have just considered should be being developed and entrenched. Costs should also be considered here. Is management making efforts to maintain or attain cost leadership? Managers who let costs grow and then indulge in bouts of rationalizing with associated "exceptional" costs are seldom as able as those who routinely design processes to keep costs as low as possible. One might then look at market share, the pattern of sales growth, new product development, relative margins, asset turnover, and return on equity for the company and its competitors. How have these indicators behaved over time and since current senior management took responsibility? Buffett believes that one of the most important tasks of managers is the correct allocation of capital (we will see why later) and this will be an important part of the record.

Just as important, though, is honesty. You are an investor, not a manager. Neither are you an accountant or a private detective (this does not excuse you from healthy skepticism). Managers are in a sense your partners. You provide capital in exchange for providing them with a livelihood and a reasonable likelihood of a respectable return. Anything that unbalances this relationship too far in their favor is unhealthy, be it fraud or excessive remuneration. You are also entitled to a full and frank account of problems, their likely effect and what is being done to mitigate them. Chairmen's annual reports are too often confident about the future and unapologetic about the dismal past. If they cannot be honest about problems with their investors, can you be confident that they have the skill and courage to tackle them? A good question to ask yourself is if you would be happy to trust these people with your money in other circumstances – as a financial advisor, say, or a friend asking for a small business loan.

> We are attempting to build a model that estimates intrinsic value independent of current market price, its history, or volatility. Therefore, we do not use share-price history to assess management's ability but the underlying business performance.

3. Does the company provide value to its shareholders?

However fine the industry, however excellent the management, the acid test for an investor is his or her return, which in this case will generally come from a combination of dividend income and capital growth. We are attempting to build a model that estimates intrinsic value independent of current market price, its history, or volatility. Therefore, we do not use share-price history to assess management's ability but the underlying business performance. Are earnings significantly higher than when they were taking into account inflation? Has this increase simply been achieved by retaining capital in the business?

5

Sources of Information

OBSERVATION

Where does one find these miraculous companies that are well managed, in growing industries, and with little competition? There are thousands of quoted securities on every developed stock market. This is an opportunity – after all, no one forces you to invest, and even if you only find a handful of great businesses, these should be enough for any portfolio constructed to last an investment lifetime. The clues are all around you. Graham said that investment is most intelligent when it is most businesslike. You must be comfortable with basic business concepts, such as the way businesses create value which was discussed in the last chapter; and with basic accounting, the language of business. But as powerful as these are common sense and powers of observation. Are people buying the product? Why? Why not something else? Could another producer supply the same thing? Better? Cheaper? And is the company you are considering making a reasonable – or better yet, good – return on its investment?

Let me give you an example. While thinking about this book I happened to be traveling through a number of countries. Being aware of Buffett's involvement, I was struck forcibly by the ubiquity of Coke – it appears to be sold on every street and up every mountain in the world. It only occurred to me slowly, however, that there was another product that seems to be almost as widely distributed – chewing gum. Most brands belong to one company, William Wrigley, and this one company appears to have dominated its markets forever. Get hold of its accounts and you will see that it passes many of the tests in this book. Why is Berkshire Hathaway not a Wrigley shareholder? I suspect that it is because the stock price is too high – there is no margin of safety.

PUBLIC INFORMATION

There are a number of straightforward ways to check your intuition. Always number one is the annual report and preferably look at a few years' worth. Most companies will deliver them on request or have made them available on the internet. How should you read it? Look for the signs of competence and honesty. How has the company coped with setbacks? Is there enough detail in the front and in the notes properly to understand how the company makes its money? From which countries or products is it getting the fastest growth and is that where new investment is going? Then look at the numbers. What is the basic story of growth, profitability, and investment? The company probably also publishes brochures which you may also be able to pick up for free that give you a better idea about the product range and likely customers. In most cases to be avoided is broker research. This is often of poor quality and concentrates on very short-term forecasting. The exceptional analysts usually only provide research to substantial investing institutions, but even then concentrate on predicting basic numbers over a few years.

In most cases to be avoided is broker research. This is often of poor quality and concentrates on very short-term forecasting.

It is no exaggeration to state that all you will usually need to invest well are annual reports, a good newspaper such as the *Financial Times* or *Wall Street Journal*, and patience.

KEY VALUE DRIVERS

Companies do not trade in money. They sell goods and services to customers. What signs are there that one company is better than any other in its industry? There are conventional ratios such as gross and operating margins, but they are often misleading because of differing accounting conventions and capital costs. Often more useful is to develop your own notion of key drivers for the industry. Say you were considering an investment in a clothes retailer. You would certainly be interested in its gross and operating margins but also how much it sells per square foot, how much it has invested per square foot, how often it sells all its stock, how often it has to pay its creditors, how much growth is coming from existing sites versus new ones and so on. You would want to look at these numbers

> There are conventional ratios such as gross and operating margins, but they are often misleading because of differing accounting conventions and capital costs. Often more useful is to develop your own notion of key drivers for the industry.

over time and how competitors fared in the same terms. Then step away from the numbers: what are they telling you and does that fit in with your observations? Do the companies' stores appear well-managed? Are they busier than their rivals? Are the locations appropriate for the strategy (main street/secondary/out-of-town)? What threats are there? Could rivals easily reproduce the best features of your company? Are there limits to growth? Will direct-mail/catalogue/online suppliers directly compete?

Buffett's key drivers – two examples

Retail

Although he has a few investments in this area Buffett is no great fan of retailers. His largest positions are in the wholly-owned Nebraska Furniture Mart (NFM) and See's Candies. His main objection to the industry is that it is quite easy for competitors to copy the leader; suppliers are not usually tied to one outlet, locations are rarely unique and customer service innovations can be imitated.

As in other industries where Buffett has no great conviction about product differentiation, he has tended to invest in the lowest-cost competitor. NFM sells more per square foot in its principal product categories than any other competitor in the USA. Its secret? Low prices. Its margins are lower than its rivals but stock turnover is higher. Low investment in space plus low investment in stock plus high sales equals a high return on investment. Munger is a director of the similar quoted company, Costco.

See's is a bit different. What gives it the edge is its fine candy and great customer service (I went in recently with a cold and was smothered in concern and free samples). These are intangibles but greatly more important than location or the salary bill. Nonetheless, Buffett has identified a volume-per-square-foot-related measure – pounds of candy sold per outlet – and diligently uses it to track See's progress. Apart from increasing its poundage sold per outlet per year, See's is able routinely to raise its prices in real terms and compared to its competitors. With commodity inputs, like sugar, much of these volume and price increases fall through to its bottom line. Effectively, Buffett uses conventional quantitative measures, such as sales per square foot, to detect qualitative advantages in See's case or cost advantages as with NFM.

Banking

Interestingly, Buffett sometimes sees banks as retailers – most have main street outlets selling commodity products in competition with many others. He has made a few small investments in this industry over the years and one big one, Wells Fargo, covered in detail as a case study (see Chapter 18).

In conventional terms, banks are actually not that easy to analyze. Most retail banks make most of their money by doing what banks have done for centuries – taking deposits and lending money, but there are deposits and deposits. Borrowing money at high rates is not nearly as profitable as sitting on individual deposit accounts that pay negligible interest, but what about the high cost of servicing thousands of small depositors from hundreds of expensive main street locations? The profitability of loans is even more difficult to assess since you won't know if an individual advance has been profitable for a long time; then if the loan does not repay, you may suffer a loss; if it does, you have lost your source of profit.

Following the familiar pattern, since most banks are similar, Buffett has tended to invest in those with a history of and commitment to low costs. His principal value driver is return on assets (net profit divided by average total assets) and he generally looks for this measure to be well above 1 per cent. (Look at the accounts of your own bank over time – it probably rarely earns much over 1 per cent on its assets.)

OTHER TRICKS OF THE TRADE

You must learn to think in competitive terms. Who are the competitors, what motivates them, who else could be attracted to this market? Look at their reports and literature, too, and if possible the products. No indignity is too great. When Buffett was first considering an investment in Disney, he went to a cinema to view the product. It only slowly dawned on him that a man in a suit looked foolish in a cinema full of kids. And when American Express was hit by a scandal in the 1960s, he got behind the cashier at local restaurants and supermarkets to check that customers were using the card and travelers cheques just as much as before.

It is possible to take this kind of on-the-ground competitive analysis further. Philip Fisher looked for scuttlebutt. By rigorously interviewing the management of the potential investee, its competitors, customers, and suppliers, he built up a solid idea of who was best at what. He summed up his agenda in 15 questions he wanted to able to answer which you will find in his *Common Stocks and Uncommon Profits*. Many of them are about the ability of the company to maintain sales growth and a couple deal with management's openness and integrity.

> When Buffett was first considering an investment in Disney, he went to a cinema to view the product. It only slowly dawned on him that a man in a suit looked foolish in a cinema full of kids.

Buffett also likes to understand his investments thoroughly. Most often, though, he does this by sitting at his desk, reading annual reports, and thinking.

6

Using What You Know, Using What You Feel

KNOW YOUR OWN LIMITS . . .

Nobody forces you to invest. A hot tip is rarely based on anything other than someone else's hunch. It is worth reading about what great long-term investors like Buffett or Peter Lynch are doing. Should you copy them you may do well, though you will never know exactly when they are buying or selling because of information time lags. But you would be learning nothing (and it would be no fun). Better to develop your own approach. Sensible investing starts with what you know, not what your broker knows, and not even what Buffett knows. But before you even decide what you do know, it is crucial to recognize what you don't. Fisher was very comfortable with the semiconductor and chemical industries. Buffett is not. He does not even own pharmaceutical stock, where it is easy to understand what sells the product, but difficult to know where long-term competitive advantage lies, unless you are an expert. Maybe you are. Remember, however, that some industries are in themselves fast-moving and difficult to forecast. Microsoft has made a fortune by dominating PC operating systems and applications markets, but there were no PCs 20 years ago. Will there be any in 20 years' time? Truthfully, nobody can answer that question. Any investment in Microsoft that depends on it continuing to produce cash at current or higher levels for 20 years or more is, therefore, a speculation, not an investment, but anybody can see that Disney or

Gillette will continue to be in business, and probably dominating their businesses, for a lifetime.

. . . BUT ALSO USE YOUR STRENGTHS

From Peter Lynch to the Beardstown Ladies, many people have written about looking for investments in your backyard. This does not mean investing because you notice that one restaurant is doing better than the one down the road or because a soap powder washes whiter, but this is an excellent place to start. I once found a great business by looking out of the window. I noticed that a courier company was making daily deliveries to the building opposite. This led to me thinking about couriers, their future demand and industry economics. Romantics will be pleased that the firm I chose to invest in owned the van I first saw (but it took me six months before I thought about it as an investment cue).

> I noticed that a courier company was making daily deliveries to the building opposite. This led to me thinking about couriers, their future demand and industry economics. Romantics will be pleased that the firm I chose to invest in owned the van I first saw (but it took me six months before I thought about it as an investment cue).

As we noted earlier, many of Buffett's best investment ideas came from businesses he has known well all of his life – Coca-Cola as a consumer, the *Washington Post* as a delivery boy. He did not need much convincing that these were great products. When he got around decades later to looking at their accounts, he noticed that they were great companies too. He then waited until the price was right.

The one-question test for understandability

Where will the company be in ten years' time?

It is not necessary to prepare ten-year cashflows to answer this question. You just must be confident that earnings will be substantially higher. This generally flows from being better than the actual and potential competition, growing sales, and controlling costs. If you cannot answer this question, do not invest.

USING WHAT YOU FEEL

Master the numbers, understand the product, its markets, and the competition. Then step back. Be honest with yourself. How well do you really feel you understand the business? Do you know why people buy the product? What is the shape of the market? Broadly speaking, who has what market share? What new products or refinements of the existing offer will be available in a year's time? In five years? What would you do to improve sales or margins? You should have some confidence in answering these questions. You should also believe that the management of the company to whom you are entrusting your money has thought as far ahead.

By investing in a company you are entering into a partnership with its managers and you take ownership of a particular history of economic relationships. Two emotional questions are relevant.

1. Are you comfortable with the products and markets?

I think it is legitimate to ask whether you really want to turn a penny off the sale of certain things. Guns and tobacco kill people, alcohol and burgers have their undesirable effects, too. As an investor you are not responsible for selling these things in the day-to-day sense, but you are morally responsible by profiting from those sales. Even Disney now faces criticism for supposedly promoting violence, gay rights, and sweatshop production. You are likely to be associated with your investments for many years, maybe decades. Are you sure you are happy with how you make your money? I should add that Buffett has invested in all the areas mentioned except, other than briefly, in tobacco.

> You are likely to be associated with your investments for many years, maybe decades. Are you sure you are happy with how you make your money?

2. Are you comfortable with the management?

We have thought about management's competence and their preparedness. What about their honesty? Are they open about problems and mistakes? Do they prepare for their own succession or are they constantly forcing out potential rivals? Similarly, do they give credit to more junior staff who may be doing the difficult work of selling and developing new products? What about remuneration? Are the profits shared fairly between staff, management, and shareholders? Buffett is not a fan of share-option schemes. They can encourage short-termism and per-share value is easily maximized by paying out no or low dividends.

The one-question test for integrity

Would you be happy to leave your money with these managers for ten years?

Your money is in trust. Others have control of it. Are you comfortable with that? Are you happy with these mangers being in control? Imagine that you were the only shareholder and that you had to go to a desert island for ten years. Will these people have grown the business in such a way that you will benefit as well as them?

7

Goodwill

If it is the case that the intrinsic value of certain enterprises exceeds the net worth on their audited balance sheet, there must be other kinds of asset that auditors are not picking up. This difference between the intrinsic value and book value is called "goodwill". This is a much used word meaning different things in different contexts. The most common alternative use is the difference between the acquisition price of a company and its book value. The former meaning, which we will be using in this chapter, we will call *economic goodwill*, the latter *acquired goodwill*.

All businesses need tangible assets of the sort that are audited. However, the kind of factors we have seen lead to unusual profitability – management drive, great customer or supplier relationships, pricing power – never turn up on the accounts. Boiling down the insights of Buffett, Fisher, and Porter, we have seen that economic goodwill is often generated where excellent management and favorable industry conditions are combined. The kind of industry meant is one where there is rising demand or otherwise favorable circumstances (Buffett calls this a tailwind) and some restriction on all-out competitive war. This may arise from restrictions on new entrants, a strongly entrenched market position or an enduring low-cost advantage. Apart from the value-driver analysis and comfort factors outlined in the last two chapters, what purely financial clues are there that economic goodwill has been created?

> **This difference between the intrinsic value and book value is called "goodwill".**

OTHER PEOPLE'S MONEY — SOURCES OF CAPITAL

Businesses need assets, such as premises and stocks, in order to trade. To finance them they raise cash from a number of sources, principally shareholders, lenders, and suppliers. A few lucky companies are financed by their customers, as magazines are by their subscribers. For much of the past century the most favored companies on stock markets were those with the most assets relative to earnings, notably railroads, banks, car manufacturers, steel, and textile mills. The other side of the Graham coin, a company rich in these types of assets, was regarded as solid, its share price well-backed with something tangible. Buffett's main holding company, Berkshire Hathaway, started as this sort of enterprise with highly valued factories and plant but low earnings or losses.

What happens when this kind of business tries to grow? Let's create an example:

Heavy Holdings

Balance sheet			
Cash	0	Debt	0
Stock	5	Suppliers	12
Debtors	7		
Factories and plant	100	Shareholders' funds	100
Total assets	112	Total liabilities	112
Profit and loss			
Turnover	70		
Profit after tax	5		

Heavy Holdings trots along and over the next decade manages to double its earnings, a less than spectacular 7 per cent p.a. However, the likelihood is that to grow earnings even at this rate its turnover will have also doubled. And to double its sales it will probably have had to double the nominal value of its stock, debtors, and fixed assets.

At the start of the decade its *operating assets* (the stock, debtors and fixed assets minus credit obtained from suppliers necessary to run the business) totaled 100 (5 + 7 + 100 – 12). At the end of the decade it will need operating assets of 200 (say, stock of 10, debtors of 14, fixed assets of 200 and suppliers' credit of 24). Even if it has paid no dividends the total of ten years' retained earnings is barely 75. But its operating assets have increased by 100. Merely to survive it must borrow 25 or issue new equity with this value. This is clearly unsustainable since over time it will reach a limit to how much it can borrow or the original shareholders' stake will be diluted to a worthless value. There is another way of showing that Heavy is destroying value. Imagine that you believe that all businesses are worth the same earnings multiple, say, ten. You would say that Heavy is worth ten times profits, 50, at the beginning and 100 at the end of this period. So the value of the business has increased by 50, but as a shareholder you have had to support the business with 100 of fresh investment. For every 2 of your money that the business has retained, it has created only 1 in value.

We might say that Heavy is an example of a business possessing *economic badwill*; it is worth more dead than alive, so its intrinsic value is below its balance sheet book value. Of course, someone *might* come along and pay book value or management *might* liquidate under-performing assets – in practice they often do not.

Light Holdings

Balance sheet

Cash	0	Debt	0
Stock	5	Suppliers	12
Debtors	7		
Factories and plant	20	Shareholders' funds	20
Total assets	32	Total liabilities	32

Profit and loss

Turnover	70
Profit after tax	5

Light has exactly the same trading margins as Heavy, but it makes do with substantially fewer assets. Say Light experiences the same growth as

Heavy for ten years. It will also end up with doubled turnover and profits. The chances are it will also have twice as much tied up in operating assets. They totaled 20, now 40, so a net 20 will have been reinvested. Generated profits will have exceeded 75 in the period and only 20 needed to be retained; therefore c.55 cash (plus the interest earned on this 55) will be on the balance sheet or have been paid out in dividends. Again making the assumption that the business is worth 50 at the start and 100 at the end plus the 55 cash, value of 105 has been created compared to the 20 investment, or 5 generated for every 1 retained.

UNEQUAL EARNINGS

What exactly was it about Heavy that made it such a champion creator of badwill? For one thing it ran out of cash or the ability to raise cash even though it was not growing fast. The average business is not in quite the same state as Heavy. But it is rarely able to sustain Light's enviable economics for long either. In fact, many businesses are unable to grow at even a modest rate without retaining a substantial part of their earnings. As we saw in the two examples, the important question is not whether you retain earnings, as almost all growing businesses have to do, but how well they are reinvested. Heavy needed to reinvest all its profits and more but destroyed value in the process. Light needed to reinvest a portion of its profits, but was both able to create value with this investment and generate cash.

> **Almost all of Buffett's equity investments can be summed up as follows: they are growing companies that can reinvest capital at highly attractive rates of return.**

How do you know if a given business can do this? Well, every business has a history of reinvestment and a history of returns. These are conveniently summarized in one measure, *return on equity* (ROE).

ROE is defined as profits after tax or net income divided by the average of shareholders' funds employed during the year. We shall amplify this definition and its importance in the following chapters. Generally speaking, though, the *total shareholders' funds number*, also known as net worth, book value, or book equity, is the sum total of the share-holders' commitment to the business, both the initial investment and subsequently retained earnings. And *net income* is the profit available to shareholders from this investment.

Using ROE one can very quickly tell if a business is like Light or Heavy. Correcting for debt/cash balances, most companies over time find it difficult to exceed an ROE of c.10–12 per cent. It is easy to understand why. A business demonstrating a ROE of, say, 15 per cent will attract competitors willing to invest for this kind of future return, which is better than it could achieve on cash deposits or by investing in an average business. Only companies with Buffett characteristics will be able to repel these com-petitors and maintain a high ROE. It is crucial to remember that a high ROE is only interesting inasmuch as it is a pre-dictor of a continuing ability to invest at high rates.

> Every business has a history of reinvestment and a history of returns. These are conveniently summarized in one measure, *return on equity* (ROE). ROE is defined as profits after tax or net income divided by the average of shareholders' funds employed during the year.

One moral from this analysis is that not all earnings are equal. A Heavy type of enterprise must reinvest all of its earnings or stop grow-ing. Even the average company earning 10 per cent on its equity is *compelled* to direct a large part of its generated cash to reinvestment, whether it wants to or not. It is an insight of Buffett's that every ven-ture has two parts. There is the business itself declaring a profit and there is the fate of that profit. Heavy type businesses have no choice but to reinvest. Average businesses can either reinvest, but for average returns, or stop growing. Light type businesses must also reinvest but earn superior returns for doing so *and* throw off surplus cash.

TAX AND INFLATION

What is interesting to the investor is his or her total return. Taxes are a vital and unavoidable fact of investment. It is, therefore, the total after-tax return of alternative investment opportunities that must be considered. This is a factor in Buffett's wish to find companies that can grow in the long term, that is, where a large part of the value will manifest in an appreciating share price rather than a dividend stream, and taxes can be postponed until the shares are sold, that is indefinitely. Since the principal taxes are neutral between stocks and other securities, tax has rarely been influential in attracting or repelling Buffett to or from stocks as a class.

As strong a macro influence on Buffett has been the postwar phenomenon of periodic severe inflation. General price inflation has several times decimated the value of cash, government securities, and other bonds. Fixed interest rates of 3 per cent which looked handsome 40 years ago will have drastically reduced the real value of many families' portfolios in living memory (a 10 per cent inflation will halve the value of a 3 per cent bond in ten years). A business happily producing a 10 per cent ROE will also only mark time in earnings terms if inflation is 10 per cent (and will decline in value if dividends attract tax). Furthermore, whether or not volume is growing, *all* of its earnings will be forced into reinvestment. As much as any other factor it was the periodic reemergence of inflation that led Buffett back to ROE.

> **What is interesting to the investor is his or her total return. Taxes are a vital and unavoidable fact of investment. It is, therefore, the total after-tax return of alternative investment opportunities that must be considered.**

STOCKS AS BONDS

If many companies over time cannot increase their return to equity they can be thought of as a special sort of bond: a perpetual with a coupon fluctuating around 10–12 per cent available to pay out in cash or to be reinvested at much the same rate. When conventional government or corporate bonds are paying a 5 or 7 per cent rate one might be tempted to pay a good premium to book value for such stocks. However, the constant risk of a resurgence in inflation would likely drive the interest rate receivable on bonds toward or beyond the 10 per cent level. In an essay Buffett wrote in 1977, he demonstrated that, contrary to the then widely held belief, inflation of itself would not increase the return on equity that companies could earn. In other words, inflation will tend to increase the average bond coupon but leave the average stock coupon (ROE) unchanged. There is, therefore, always a risk that the premium to book to which stockholders are accustomed will be extinguished: the average stock may over time possess no goodwill.

8

Capital Allocation

Buffett's often repeated maxim that one of the most important tasks of senior management is capital allocation now makes sense. Even an apparently growing business can be creating economic badwill if the growth both requires reinvested capital and the returns on that capital are poor. A common parallel that he uses is a savings account. If the interest rate obtainable is 10 per cent and all income is reinvested, earnings will also grow 10 per cent every year. There is no magic about this, but many managers are lauded for achieving no more after years of leading large enterprises.

Other than reinvestment in the core activity, there are several important ways in which company management can deploy its capital to create goodwill or badwill: diversification and acquisition; dividends and retention; and debt policy.

DIVERSIFICATION AND ACQUISITION

Berkshire Hathaway is one of the most diversified large companies in existence today. Although its main business is insurance, it also sells furniture, jewelry, newspapers, steel, encyclopaedias, and vacuum cleaners. It has grown strongly organically and by acquisition. Warren Buffett is nonetheless critical of the general run of acquisitive or diversified companies. He believes that many expansions serve managers' egos and wallets but rarely reward shareholders. Even excellent businesses are prone to unnecessary diversification, often encouraged by consultants or investment bankers with a vested interest in doing deals. Also responsible are the academics who claim that diversification is necessary to reduce risk. Buffett is as dismissive of companies assembling a range of unrelated subsidiaries for this reason as he is of investors building up a large portfolio of stocks to minimize volatility.

> Buffett reserves special contempt for companies which buy other companies and routinely offer their own shares in payment. His basic test is that what is being bought should be worth more than what is being used for payment.

In fact, Buffett believes managers should apply the same criteria to acquisitions or new ventures as he applies to his investments: Do we understand this business? Is it well-run, or can we supply management? Is the price below intrinsic value? If they did, far fewer acquisitions would be made.

Buffett reserves special contempt for companies which buy other companies and routinely offer their own shares in payment. His basic test is that what is being bought should be worth more than what is being used for payment. His experience is that paper-issuing companies often end up enriching the vendors of businesses they buy and impoverishing their own shareholders. Over the 30 and more years of its current management Berkshire Hathaway's market and book values have increased by more than a thousandfold; shares in issue by 8 per cent.

DIVIDENDS AND RETENTIONS

Almost all growing businesses need to retain earnings (in the last chapter this was true of Light as well as Heavy). Those with a high ROE should be able to produce cash as well. A complacent or weak management will squander the cash that is thrown off a high-return business on expensive acquisitions or stockpile cash in the bank. The latter is preferable to wasting it but still not as shareholder-friendly as handing it back. The worst consequence of holding onto cash is that the company becomes complacent and costs rise unnecessarily, allowing competitors in with lower prices.

Companies should always have enough cash on hand to avoid pressure from creditors over a business cycle. Acquisitions are also perfectly acceptable as long as they strictly add more intrinsic value than their cost. In most cases shareholders benefit from getting their money back as dividends which can be invested elsewhere.

The increasingly popular share buy-back is an odd form of dividend. The company uses its cash to buy its own shares back from investors. Again the value test is that the company should pay less for each share than its own per-share intrinsic value. Buffett loves this. Since he rarely tenders his own shares for sale, he ends up with a higher per centage ownership of outstanding shares in a company whose management has proven itself to be shareholder-oriented. The most startling illustration of this is GEICO. Berkshire bought 33.3 per cent of the company in the late 1970s for $45.7 million. GEICO's earnings grew strongly and it was also a prodigious cash producer. It used surplus cash to buy its own shares such that by 1995 Berkshire owned 50 per cent of the business, never having bought another share directly. Berkshire then paid $2.3 billion for the other half of the company.

Share buy-backs have recently taken off in the name of "shareholder value". For most companies trading at high multiples of earnings, they are probably destroying value: just as it makes sense if one can buy $1 for 50 cents it is stupid to pay $2 for $1. My suspicion is that many managements initiate buy-backs because they realize that they enhance earnings per share, whereas dividends have the opposite effect. For these companies buy-backs are simply an expensive way of indebting themselves, which brings us to our next consideration.

> Companies should always have enough cash on hand to avoid pressure from creditors over a business cycle. Acquisitions are also perfectly acceptable as long as they strictly add more intrinsic value than their cost.

> The increasingly popular share buy-back is an odd form of dividend. The company uses its cash to buy its own shares back from investors. Again the value test is that the company should pay less for each share than its own per-share intrinsic value.

DEBT POLICY

Buffett is keen on a high ROE, but not if the price is high borrowing. In fact, many businesses can increase their apparent returns to shareholders merely by gearing up. The cost of this policy is not just the interest bill but the risk that cashflow will be disrupted one year and the company will default. One should not mind a variable stream of earnings as long as the average and sustainable return to equity is high. Too much debt brings a certain risk that the enterprise will cease to exist altogether. Overall debt levels should be low, measured both on interest cover grounds and by what a normal lender would be comfortable with. Return on equity should be measured on the operating assets of the business, what assets and liabilities it needs for normal purposes, including a little cash or debt if appropriate. An example of a business that has apparently achieved a high ROE, but is in fact relying on ever higher borrowings, is General Electric.

9

Return on Equity

We have seen that Buffett regards this as the central measure of financial well-being. Goodwill is the premium to book value which a business is worth if it has the ability to earn high returns on reinvested equity. An average company producing, say, a 10 per cent ROE over time may be worth a premium to its book value in a time of low interest rates, but interest rates move in cycles and that premium may soon be extinguished.

Buffett finds it safer to hunt for businesses with exceptional ROEs that are likely to recur and will far exceed ordinary bond or cash returns. Let us turn back to the stock as bond explanation. We saw that a stock reliably returning 10 per cent to equity may broadly be worth as much as a 10 per cent bond. There are two important differences. First, most bonds have a maturity, that is a date on which the original capital is returned or a new rate can be negotiated. Equities are perpetual. Unless you are a controlling shareholder you are at the mercy of management who may or may not return a dividend or reinvest generated cash. The second difference is related. It has to do with what in standard corporate finance theory is called reinvestment risk.

> **Goodwill is the premium to book value which a business is worth if it has the ability to earn high returns on reinvested equity.**

Reinvestment risk is the chance that you will not be able to invest the income produced by a security advantageously even though the terms of the investment appear fixed. If you buy a conventional 10 per cent bond and you are happy with the credit risk, you can be sure that every year until maturity you will receive an income equal to 10 per cent of your original capital. What you cannot know is what that income will be able to afford when it periodically arrives. One can neither know what inflation will have taken the price of real goods to nor what prevailing interest rates will have done to the price of securities. This is not an academic question. Under most reasonable assumptions the value of the income from such a bond will far exceed the original investment after ten years. Say interest rates fall before the first year's income is received, 10 per cent bonds will now cost a lot more. It is impossible to forecast one's total long-term return.

Buffett's subtle mind turned this upside down. If one considers an equity to be a disguised perpetual bond capable of producing a fixed return on equity, one has what might be called "reinvestment opportunity". Equities pay dividends and this element (or rather how one can redeploy this element) is still unpredictable. But the retained part of earnings will be reinvested at a fairly knowable rate – ROE. If the sustainable ROE is 10 per cent retained earnings will also earn 10 per cent. The normal bond pays out 100 per cent of its "earnings" as income. Most companies pay out 50 per cent or less. A high ROE company, growing reasonably fast and maybe buying back shares may pay a very low share of its earnings out in cash.

> **Reinvestment risk** is the chance that you will not be able to invest the income produced by a security advantageously even though the terms of the investment appear fixed.

> **Reinvestment opportunity** is the option a growing business has to reinvest large proportions of its generated capital at high rates of return. Businesses with such an opportunity produce the most goodwill.

This is the fundamental financial truth underlying most of Buffett's investments. American Express's ROE is 23 per cent, Gillette's over 35 per cent and Coca-Cola's a mind-boggling 55 per cent. In each of these cases this return is rising. (Bear in mind the strong corollary of the margin of safety. Even these remarkable businesses have a value and Buffett is determined to pay less.)

To sum up, ROE is important because it gives a clue as to how well a business can reinvest its earnings. A business with a sustainable ROE of 20 per cent not only produces an income relative to investment twice as high as an average stock or bond; it may give you the opportunity, through reinvestment, to own a perpetual stream of 20 per cent returns. The ultimate company, which can reinvest all of its earnings at this rate

> If one considers an equity to be a disguised perpetual bond capable of producing a fixed return on equity, one has what might be called "reinvestment opportunity".

for a long time into the future will effectively give you a compounded 20 per cent return on your initial investment.

How to calculate ROE

There are two parts to ROE: *net income* and *equity*. From net income it is important to remember to deduct income going to other parties: tax obviously, but also preference dividends, the present cost of earn-outs on acquisitions and the cost of equity options granted to management. Most exceptional costs and income can be ignored. Bear in mind, though, that companies making "exceptional" provisions for cost-cutting projects are probably in competition with better-managed businesses routinely keeping down cost. Add back the amortization of acquired goodwill which is not a real cost to business at all but an arbitrary accounting adjustment. Depreciation, however, while not paid in cash is a real and hard cost. It should always be deducted unless equivalent adjustments are being made to capital expenditure (see below).

Buffett has developed concepts called "owner earnings" and "look-through earnings". Apart from net income, they take into account two other effects. If a business owns a minority of another company it may only be able to show its dividend income on the face of its accounts. The underlying earnings of that minority stake may be higher. Berkshire's ownership of 10.5 per cent of American Express's (Amex) common equity in 1996 gave it ownership of 10.5 per cent of Amex's net income, $190 million. $44 million of this was paid out in dividends and the rest was reinvested. Berkshire's accounts only reflected the amount received in dividends. Look-through earnings include the whole underlying amount.

The idea of owner earnings applies to all conventional businesses. It is an attempt to adjust net income for other routine cashflow effects. As we have seen, simply to grow with inflation and even without volume growth, most companies need to reinvest earnings in higher amounts of working and fixed capital. By adding back depreciation to net income and subtracting the investment required in capital without volume growth, owner earnings estimates the true income in cash terms that a business is generating. In practice, it is quite difficult to separate the required investment from the investment for growth. What we have seen is that high ROE businesses, not relying on debt, are able to grow by reinvesting in highly productive new capital. A low ROE business like Heavy conscripts all of its earnings into new but still unproductive capital; it has low or negative owner earnings.

For our purposes, and bearing in mind that even a portion of a high ROE business's earnings are reserved for necessary reinvestment, we will use net income rather than owner earnings in our calculations.

The equity side of the calculation is not nearly so straightforward. There are minor questions of definition, such as deducting preference shares, minority interests, and bought-in shares/treasury stock; and unless there has been a large capital raising in the year the average equity total should be used. The big issues involve intangible assets, such as acquired goodwill, patents, and media rights. Acquired goodwill is a very tricky one since no single treatment is quite right. Include it and you may overestimate the amount of ongoing capital needed to support operating assets and, therefore, underestimate the true return. Exclude it and you may be ignoring the possibility that a lot of cash has been paid for a low return – the ROE will be much higher than it should be. Wells Fargo is a good example. Historically it had been able to generate an ROE of 30 per cent. In 1996 it bought another substantial banking group for $11.3 billion, of which $9.4 billion was goodwill or other intangibles. 1996 stated ROE plummeted to 9 per cent. Adding back goodwill amortization to net income but leaving book equity as stated brings ROE to 13 per cent. Taking the intangibles of the equity base rockets ROE back to 38 per cent, but this can't be right. If Wells had paid another $1 billion in shares its after intangible equity base would have been still lower and its ROE even higher – but nothing about the underlying businesses would have changed.

There is an answer to this conundrum and it involves looking at the incremental cash returns only of fresh investment. This will be explored in the next chapter.

OTHER TYPES OF BUSINESS

There are some industries where it is difficult to apply ROE analysis even though over long periods of time their returns to equity may be equal to any other activity. Insurance companies fall into the first of the look-through earnings traps described above. A large part of their assets may be held as equities where the only annual reported income is dividends. Earnings retained by these individual investee companies will eventually manifest themselves as future dividends or capital gains, but the latter in particular may be irregular and unpredictable. Berkshire Hathaway has this problem although since it owns far fewer equities than the average insurance company it is easier to make look-through estimates.

Property companies and other businesses that hold assets for a long time and hope to make capital gains, such as venture capitalists, are similarly resistant to easy ROE analysis.

10

IP: The Incremental Principle

We saw in the last chapter how goodwill and other intangible assets could make ROE analysis tricky. There are other times when the historic balance sheet can be misleading. Companies where a lot of the capital is historic may appear to be making excellent equity returns, but as soon as the capital needs replacing, ROE will fall. Where there have been losses in the company's history this will also depress the equity base and apparently boost the return. So it goes on. The way out of this impasse is to recall that it is the return that the business can generate out of additional capital in which we are really interested.

Understanding the concept behind ROE was pretty easy – simply the total current return compared to the total historic investment. Getting hold of the most recent result is not much more difficult. We are looking for the improvement in return compared to the increased investment needed to provide that return. This is still not a forecast of future ROE but it is more up-to-date than the measure we have been using so far. It can also smooth us over the accounting problems mentioned above. I call this measure IP: the incremental principle, which is:

$$\frac{\text{Adjusted Net Income, Year 2} - \text{Adjusted Net Income, Year 1}}{\text{Shareholders' Equity, End Year 2} - \text{Shareholders' Equity, Beginning Year 2}}$$

Note: Adjusted Net Income is the profit after tax and preference dividends but before ordinary dividends and adjusted for exceptional items.

In the following example a business has been bought at a premium of 50 to its book value. This acquired goodwill has been written off.

Goodwill Limited

Year	1	2	3
Goodwill	(50)	(50)	(50)
Fixed assets	30	33	36
Net current assets	20	22	24
Net assets	50	55	60
Net income	10	10.5	11
Return on average equity	20%	19%	
IP	10%	10%	

The initial ROE looks impressive at 20 per cent. However, the IP tells the true story. Profits are only growing at 0.5 p.a. but require 5 to be reinvested in operating assets each year giving a 10 per cent incremental return. If this performance were to be extended at the same rate, ROE would eventually also fall to 10 per cent. This picture is in fact fairly typical of an acquisitive conglomerate appearing to reap high returns from each conquest but pretty soon slowing down; only another purchase will reinvigorate apparent returns.

> **Understanding the concept behind ROE was pretty easy – simply the total current return compared to the total historic investment. Getting hold of the most recent result is not much more difficult.**

Another familiar story is told by our next example.

Start-up Limited

Year	1	2	3
Fixed assets	120	123	127
Net current assets	80	82	84
Net assets	200	205	211
Net income	10	12	14
Return on average equity		6%	7%
IP	40%	33%	

Many start-up companies or businesses new to an industry display the above pattern. You will particularly notice it in sectors like hotels or heavy industry where substantial capital expenditure only pays off as capacity is utilized. Note the rapid increase in net income, 15–20 per cent p.a. When you look at the ROE and IP ratios you realize this seeming income boom is merely catch-up. If the 200 initially invested had gone into the bank, it would have produced a better result in each of the three years.

Another good rule for finding Buffettesque stocks is, therefore:

Return on equity should be high and sustainably high. The incremental return on incremental equity, IP, should also be high.

BEYOND THE INCREMENTAL PRINCIPLE

IP is very useful for estimating sustainable ROE where the balance sheet is unclear. To work, though, there must be increases in both profit and shareholders' funds in the year in question. Where profits are flat or declining, the key is to determine whether this is permanent or not; it may still be possible to estimate the underlying increase, but there are obvious risks if income continues to decline. Shareholders' funds rarely reduce other than because of major asset write-downs, losses, or share repurchases. Again, one must be cautious – if the write-down is independent of trading, one could write it back for the IP calculation, but asset provisions often conceal trading problems.

> IP is very useful for estimating sustainable ROE where the balance sheet is unclear. To work, though, there must be increases in both profit and shareholders' funds in the year in question.

An interesting side question is what to do if growing businesses need to retain no more capital. It does not happen often. Businesses like American Express or GEICO that suck in customers' deposits or premiums in advance of declaring profits are candidates. IP would be impossible to use since the shareholders' investment would be declining and one would have to rely on ROE alone.

11

Estimating Value

It is time to summarize the steps we have taken so far.

- Good businesses to own are ones where we understand the product and why demand for it will grow. Management is honest and able. The business should possess a sustainable advantage over its rivals such that new entrants are deterred, existing competitors are outpaced, and there is pricing power against customers and suppliers. The best investment would be in an unregulated monopoly, but otherwise the company is likely to have an unshakeable niche or enduring low costs.
- The average company produces 10–12 per cent p.a. returns to equity over time. Bonds currently yield less but the recurrence of inflation means that they will earn more, and perhaps more than stocks, from time to time. Therefore, while it is often legitimate for the average stock to have an intrinsic value above book, that is, possess goodwill, that premium may not endure.
- Companies that can sustain a high ROE possess enduring economic goodwill. Moreover, if the business can employ large amounts of retained capital and maintain those returns, that goodwill will multiply.

THE DISCOUNT RATE

The last piece of the jigsaw is the discount rate, the rate to which we are comparing the sustainable ROE. Forests have been sacrificed by academics to justify different cost of capital calculations. Buffett takes a much simpler approach. At times he has suggested using the long government bond rate. This fluctuates itself though and who are we to forecast it? The evidence is he uses 10 per cent and supplies capital to his subsidiaries at 15 per cent pre-tax which comes to much the same thing. The important point is to employ a heavy margin of safety on the valuation so it will not make an enormous difference if you use 8, 9, or 10 per cent. Since investment should be made in the security with the largest margin of safety, this ranking will also be independent of the actual discount rate.

INTRINSIC VALUE

You have found a company which you believe can employ fresh capital at a sustainable return of 20 per cent p.a. There are two ways of estimating its intrinsic value. First, you can build a model of future profits and cashflow and discount the results back to today at 10 per cent p.a. This is very difficult to do in practice and often produces absurdly high valuations as conceivable investment horizons are exaggerated; or you can follow the approach that we have adopted so far and consider the stock as a bond.

We are assuming that general interest rates have a predilection for settling around 10 per cent. A straight 10 per cent bond would, therefore, normally sell for its capital or book value. A 20 per cent bond would sell for twice as much, e.g. a bond producing $5 income each year for a long period of time issued at a par of $25 would pretty soon attract buyers at $50, double par. The 20 per cent stock goes one better. It pays out some of its earnings in cash, like a bond, but the rest are retained. If it can retain earnings and sustain its 20 per cent ROE, it is like a new kind of bond, one which gives you the option of buying new 20 per cent bonds at par: for every $1 of income the business retains it can produce $0.2 p.a. of future income or $2 of value. Roughly speaking, the earnings it retains are worth double a normal company's earnings. In the general case the retained earnings of a company are worth the ratio of IP to generally available interest rates. The derived value of earnings must then again be discounted to produce intrinsic value (IV).

$$\text{Intrinsic value} = \frac{\text{Earnings} \times \text{Sustainable ROE or IP}}{(\text{Discount rate})^2}$$

Since we are assuming a long-term discount rate of 10 per cent, this is the same as saying that IV is 100 times earnings times the sustainable ROE. ROE itself is usually expressed as a per centage, so a useful shorthand is:

The intrinsic value of a security lies where its P/E equals its ROE.

MARGIN OF SAFETY

Estimating a security's value is only one half of the deal. When we invest in a publicly quoted security we are bringing nothing to the table but our right to sell. Our purchase adds no value to the company. There is, therefore, no point in paying $1 for $1.

Say we find an average company returning 10 per cent to its equity. In this example it retains all its earnings and continues to grow at 10 per cent p.a.:

Historic earnings	Current earnings	Future earnings
11.3 12.4 13.6	15	16.5 18.2

We estimate intrinsic value to be:

$$\text{IV} = \frac{15 \times 0.1}{(0.1)^2} = 150 \text{ or a p/e of 10}$$

This is also the market price, which in this case we pay. Since future earnings continue to rise 10 per cent each year on an equity base rising at the same rate, ROE will remain 10 per cent. It is quite likely that IV and market price will keep step and also increase at 10 per cent, but future rises in market price should be discounted *by* 10 per cent p.a. to give present value. We paid 150 in the current year and in two years the price will be 182, *also* worth 150 today $(182/(1.1)^2)=150)$. In sum, paying intrinsic value means we can expect no increase in real terms in the value of the investment.

> **Margin of safety simply means that we should pay as big a discount as possible to a security's intrinsic value.**

Margin of safety simply means that we should pay as big a discount as possible to a security's intrinsic value. This approach has three big advantages. Most straightforwardly we should profit over time:

1 Either the market, that is other investors, will recognize the underlying value and the market price will rise or we sit tight and benefit from the company's underlying cashflow as earnings and dividends increase;

2 We do not have to worry about the overall direction of the stockmarket. A security possesses a good margin of safety or it doesn't. The market as a whole may be crashing but over time the wellchosen security will appreciate;

3 A margin of safety is an insurance policy against our own ability and the pitfalls of the world. Management may stumble, products are recalled, our forecasting is cockeyed – a good investor will have left enough room in the purchase price such that even a poor investment will at worst not lose him or her money.

Margin of safety brings an additional comfort. You have bought into a stock at a price that you believe is well below its true value. The share price falls. Instead of worrying about the paper loss, you realize that the market has given you an opportunity to buy at an even bigger discount.

> **What is a good margin to intrinsic value? Buffett often writes about the virtues of paying 50 cents for one dollar. We will see in the case studies that he often has paid roughly 50 per cent of intrinsic value, but as with the discount rate, the precise quantum does not matter.**

What is a good margin to intrinsic value? Buffett often writes about the virtues of paying 50 cents for one dollar. We will see in the case studies that he often has paid roughly 50 per cent of intrinsic value, but as with the discount rate, the precise quantum does not matter. If you pay considerably less than the true value of a security and hold on to it, good things will happen.

I have used the word "security" in this section rather than "stock" because the concepts of value and safety are as applicable to bonds, cash, property or fine art. Your job as an investor is to find the most undervalued investment that you understand and stick with it. Buffett knows stocks and sometimes strays into bonds. Maybe you know something different.

WHEN TO SELL

Graham was prepared to sell if the market price for the security exceeded its calculated intrinsic value. Fisher is reluctant to sell unless he finds he was mistaken about the company in some objective way, but is prepared reluctantly to do so if a more attractive investment opportunity comes along. Buffett, too, will sell if he has made a mistake. He rarely liquidates merely to catch another opportunity. One reason is tax. We saw in Chapter 2 that deferring capital gains taxes gives a substantial advantage compared to regularly taking profits. More central to Buffett's philosophy is that there is more sense in sticking to the company you know than chasing phantom high returns elsewhere. In an important sense the margin of safety gets higher as your familiarity with the potential of a business develops.

> In an important sense the margin of safety gets higher as your familiarity with the potential of a business develops.

Just occasionally, sentiment intrudes. The original textile trade of Berkshire Hathaway motored on for 21 years following Buffett's investment. While it wavered between profit and loss, it never became an attractive business again. Buffett did not shut it down in this period because he felt a commitment to the staff and the communities they lived in – *and* there was a modest cash contribution after investment. When the latter became untrue and was unlikely to change, he shut it down.

Some of the major enterprises in which Berkshire holds a minority stake have been labeled "permanent holdings" by Buffett. In 1991 he wrote that the then four largest investments, Capital Cities/ABC,

Coca-Cola, GEICO, and the *Washington Post* would be held indefinitely. Since then Berkshire has bought the whole of GEICO and it remains an investor in the other three; Capital Cities was bought by Disney and Berkshire took Disney stock in that transaction. Buffett has also said that none of the wholly-owned businesses is for sale.

PART 4

CASE STUDIES

12

The American Express Company

Berkshire Hathaway bought $300 million of convertible preference shares issued by American Express Company (Amex) in 1991. These automatically converted into 14 million common shares in 1994. Berkshire bought a further 13.8 million of the common for $424 million in 1994 and 21.7 million for $669 million in 1995; a per share price of $21.40, $30.80, and $30.80 respectively.

HISTORY

Amex has reinvented itself for each American era. It was formed by a number of existing competitors in the New York express-parcel market in 1850. The two leading managers were Henry Wells and William Fargo, who went on to found California-based rival Wells, Fargo and Company in 1852. Supporting the pioneers exploiting the country's great resources, Amex had opened 4000 offices in 19 states by 1880. Like Wells, Fargo it saw another way to beat the Post Office, which launched money orders in the 1880s. Amex's product was the travelers check, invented in 1891, producing a turnover in 1892 of almost $0.5 million.

Although the company was nationalized with other express parcel services in the First World War, it was reformed shortly afterwards, with a new division. Not content with merely supplying checks, it used its overseas offices and solid reputation to promote a wide range of travel services, including travel agency and currency exchange. The offices abroad were soon swamped by the growing number of American tourists discovering the world, courtesy of cheap travel.

The boldest product extension came in 1958. There had been company accounts and credit cards for decades. Diners Card had been signing up independent restaurants since 1950, charging cardholders a fee and merchants a "discount" (a per centage of the bill). Amex saw an opportunity to attract wealthy individuals and company accounts in this market, both of which were mainstays of their travel businesses. Prelaunch publicity was huge and at the official launch date the American Express card had 250 000 applicants for "membership" and 17 000 willing merchants. Although the 1960s saw competition from the consortium-bank-owned Visa and Mastercard, Amex maintained its lead in the higher spending wealthy individual and corporate segments. Additionally, its charge card versus the other credit cards offered only a limited credit period to less risky clients; bad-debt charges were low. $2.3 billion was charged to American Express cards in 1970. As with its checks, Amex had used its reputation to wean Americans off cash.

> **Amex has reinvented itself for each American era. It was formed by a number of existing competitors in the New York express-parcel market in 1850. The two leading managers were Henry Wells and William Fargo, who went on to found California-based rival Wells, Fargo and Company in 1852.**

Under the stewardship of James Robinson, from 1977 to 1993, the core businesses grew but diversification frittered away cashflow. The then fashionable idea of a "financial supermarket," where customers could satisfy all of their financial needs, led to the acquisition of the investment bank, Shearson Loeb Rhoades, in 1991, and a whole string of brokerages and other businesses thereafter. Profits and the share price stagnated.

The Personal Connection

One of the brokerages Robinson bought was IDS. This was one of Warren Buffett's earliest stock purchases. In 1953 he bought in when its p/e was 3. He wrote a long report on the company and sold copies for $1 through an ad in the Wall Street Journal.

In the mid-60s Amex was hit by the so-called "salad-oil scandal." It had been storing containers of salad oil and issuing receipts which, on *the strength of its name, could be traded on as financial instruments. Sadly, some of the containers contained no oil; Amex had been conned. The company made sure no innocent third parties lost out at great cost to itself and Wall Street savaged the shares. The Buffett Partnership jumped in, buying 5 per cent of the stock for $13 million, 40 per cent of the partnership's total capital. This was one of Buffett's earliest attempts to find value in intangibles. He stood behind the cash register at local restaurants and visited local banks and noted that customers were using their American Express cards and checks just as frequently as before the "scandal". He compared the cost of this incident to a dividend posted by the company but never received by the stockholders. In other words, there was a one-off cost that did not affect the likely value of future earnings. Great businesses temporarily in trouble, like GEICO and Wells Fargo, have been a recurring theme since this first Amex purchase.*

AMERICAN EXPRESS IN 1991

This was the end of the Robinson era. The 1990 results were terrible. Restructuring charges and losses at the investment banking and bro-kerage unit, now called Shearson Lehman Brothers, cost $966 million. The company as a whole reported net income of $181 million, down from $1.2 billion in 1989. $890 million was raised in a common stock offering and $200 million from a convertible preferred issue. Notwithstanding these attempts to rebuild the balance sheet, Amex's credit rating was downgraded in 1991, a problem for a company whose chief virtue was undoubted financial strength.

Does the company provide value to its customers?

Amex's operations in 1990 were split as follows:

$ Millions	Net income	ROE (%)
Travel Related Services	956	28.1
American Express Bank	111	19.2
IDS	207	14.5
ISC	103	21.8
Shearson Lehman	(966)	–

IDS now mainly provided financial planning and investment advice to individuals. It had compounded its earnings 22 per cent p.a. since its acquisition in 1984, and owned or managed a mighty $51.4 billion in assets. ISC was a successful processor of other people's data, particularly credit card companies. American Express Bank had a patchy lending record, but was now focusing on wealthy individuals. Travel Related Services, which included cards, checks and travel agency, was still the heart of the company. There were now 36.5 million cards outstanding with $111 billion charged to them in 1990. That year also saw $25 billion in travelers-check sales and $5 billion in travel sales. As well as an outstanding 28 per cent ROE (although this was before allocating head office costs), this division had grown its earnings five times over ten years, or 18 per cent p.a. compound.

The marketplace was ever more crowded, however. Visa and Mastercard had been taking market share for years. Amex had also been late into the credit-card segment, where it had a tiny share, and faced severe check and travel-sale competition. From another perspective Amex still ruled. For wealthy individuals and companies, Amex was the first and often only choice for card ownership. Amex stood for strength, advice, and ubiquity. Its smaller overall market share was presented – correctly – as selectivity, so it also meant prestige. To these core customers – travelers, businessmen, restaurant patrons – use of American Express was an advertisement for themselves. American Express had achieved what few financial services companies could, customer identification with their brand.

Does the management provide value to the company?

James Robinson had many fans of whom it was reported that Buffett was one. He had grown the core businesses through reinvestment and new product development but also overextended the company.

Does the company provide value to its shareholders?

The share price had gone nowhere in five years. Not only was the profitability of the historic elements of the company being used to prop up the weaker new investments, but there was a weird dilution of shareholders' interests going on. 1990 saw $1.1 billion raised in new capital *and* $74 million common stock repurchases, *and* $413 million ordinary dividends paid (up from $359 million in 1989): bad enough to dilute existing shareholder value by being forced to issue new shares at a depressed price; absurd to hand back simultaneously to those same shareholders a great chunk in cash.

SOURCES OF INFORMATION

Buffett had known the main business and IDS for decades. But anyone could see that Amex was that unusual thing, a franchise in financial services. Let us now turn to Berkshire's first investment in 1991, a quite different decision to those taken in 1994 and 1995.

The 1991 decision

Amex continued to raise capital into 1991. Robinson contacted Buffett in the middle of the year and a week later Berkshire put up $300 million for convertible preferred shares. These paid 8.85 per cent fixed, well above the then available treasury rates of 7.5–8 per cent. Unlike the other preferred stock Berkshire was then buying (like Gillette's), this instrument was only redeemable in common stock. After three years Berkshire would exchange the preferred for a maximum 12.2 million common, subject to a maximum market value of $414 million (Berkshire could wait another year if the common was trading at less than the breakeven price of $24.50). Given that the common could theoretically be worthless, the downside was unlimited. The maximum upside, including the fixed dividend, was some 20 per cent p.a. Buffett would have been happy with the fixed-income element, but was betting that Amex was worth over $24.50 per share.

This equated to a market capitalization of $11.5 billion. The company had a proven historic ability to earn over $1 billion: net income was $1.2 billion in both 1989 and 1990 before the losses at Shearson.

Moreover, historic ROE had trended well above 20 per cent. Berkshire's small commitment was just one of a number of instances of its ability to take advantage of a low market price when a business was in temporary trouble.

The 1994 decision

In the three years up until the preferred was to be redeemed, the company took a number of large decisions at the corporate level. Robinson left the company in 1992 and was replaced by Harvey Golub, who had been previously responsible for the successful IDS unit. Golub was as determined as Robinson had been to regain market share in the card markets and focus on the key volume and profit drivers for all businesses. He realized that investment banking was a costly distraction from this task and set about selling and spinning off divisions identified as non-core. First up was ISC, the data processing arm. Great business, but what did it have to do with Amex's core values and customers? In a series of public offers Amex's investment in ISC, now renamed FDC, was reduced to 22 per cent in exchange for $2.1 billion cash. Next to go was Lehman Brothers, which was spun off to shareholders (i.e. instead of shareholders owning one piece of paper entitling them to a piece of American Express Company, which itself owned a number of businesses including Lehman, they were given two pieces of paper, one for American Express and one for Lehman). Lehman required $1.1 billion in new capital before it was deemed strong enough to have an independent existence. This was strictly a transfer from one pocket to the other, since individual Amex shareholders lost the $1.1 billion but regained it as Lehman shareholders. Prior to the spin-off in May 1994, most of the old Shearson and other brokerage businesses were also sold.

What had been happening back at base? TRS, the core historical business, had had a hard 1991 and 1992. Golub had cut the merchant discount to attract more outlets and cut back the number of cardmembers to focus on the more attractive, high-spending group. In the vogue phrase of the time the division was also "reengineered" to reduce overheads. TRS was also new to the credit card (rather than charge card) business and took some knocks before it was able to tighten its lending procedures. IDS was renamed American Express Financial Advisors (was there ever a business so fond of renaming?) and grew as steadily as before. The bank continued to bob around.

$ Millions Net income	TRS	Financial Advisors	Bank
1994	998	428	80
1993	884	358	92
1992	234	297	35
1991	396	248	60

The Financial Advisors segment was benefiting from the long-term trend for individual investors to move away from away from cash, bank deposits and institutional pensions and towards money-market funds, mutual funds, and personal pensions. Since 1990, the assets owned or managed had more than doubled to $106 billion and the earnings growth had grown 20 per cent p.a. Other key drivers – the number of planners employed and the number of clients – also grew.

TRS's improvement clearly reflected the lack of restructuring costs and bad-debt provisions in latter years. The underlying story was impressive. Amex had concentrated on signing up merchants in the industries that its high-spending clients used most: retail, oil, and travel and entertainment. There was now close to 100 per cent coverage in the latter category. There was a successful Rewards programme, offering points, goods, discounts, air miles, and the like to high spenders. On average Amex cardholders spent two and a half times as much on their cards as Visa or Mastercard owners. Particularly important because of its market share was Corporate Card business. Total card billings in 1993 were $124 billion, of which Corporate accounted for c.$34 billion. Travelers-check sales had been slowing for some years, as plastic transactions abroad replaced paper, but the business still grew, slowly, and earnings had grown to 20 per cent per annum.

QUESTIONS TO TEST YOUR UNDERSTANDING

Do you understand why people buy the product?

Amex had chiefly made money by substituting its products for cash, a habit likely to continue. It sold a slew of products connected by the brand and core values. Individuals consulting planners were relying on their skill and integrity. When they bought Amex products, such as managed funds and annuities, they were buying skill and solidity. Cardholders bought prestige and national and international presence. Check purchasers bought presence and solidity, and so on. This was quite different from the competition. They were able to match the hard facts – distribution capability and product range, for example. But it was tough to generate the soft values, what the brand stood for, without building a rival. Visa and Mastercard had presence but nothing else. Citibank and Discover had the product and distribution but no self-image.

> Amex had chiefly made money by substituting its products for cash, a habit likely to continue.

How would the industry change in the next ten years?

The Financial Advisory business was the easiest to forecast. The long-term trends we mentioned were almost bound to continue, absent a major stock-market crash. Growing job uncertainty, smaller family size, lack of a government plan and an aging population meant more self-determination in financial planning.

It was difficult to read the technological changes in TRS's markets. And there were an awful lot of new entrants attracted by the wide margins and apparent predictability of consumer lending. Amex stood above this fray slightly. If it could continue to widen its customer base without damaging its status, it could make a premium return. As a company embodying *values*, it could also benefit from technology – in a time of change people would head for where they were most comfortable.

Are you comfortable with the management?

Golub had done everything from the Buffett textbook. He got rid of poorly performing non-strategic businesses at reasonable prices. He was, therefore, only allocating capital to the strong remaining segments. He had identified the company's key drivers and concentrated on improving performance in this objective way. He had taken out cost from successful businesses when he did not need to. He had restored capital strength which was crucial to customer perception. And now that the business could support it he started on a share repurchase program.

Are there substitutes?

American Express faced competitive markets. It was not able to dominate distribution, like Gillette, and it was not the low-cost supplier, like GEICO. Where it was strong was in groups of customers, wealthy individuals, companies and travelers, in particular. These all had more money, spent more, were less price-sensitive and more brand – and value-conscious than average. Amex would have to run to keep up with these demanding types, but it had done so successfully for many decades.

FINANCIAL ANALYSIS

Amex was a hybrid company with initially confusing financial statements. To understand the profits we first must consider the balance sheet.

Consolidated balance sheet, 1993

$ Millions	December 31, 1993
Cash and investments	42 620
Receivables	16 142
Loans	14 796
Properties	1 976
Segregated assets	8 992
Other	9 606
Total assets	94 132
Customer deposits	11 131
Travelers checks	4 800
Insurance, annuity and investment certificate reserves	26 158
Debt	21 050
Segregated liabilities	8 992
Other	13 267
Shareholders' equity	8 734

First point to note is that this is a big balance sheet, that is, there are a lot of assets compared to equity. Lehman was not yet spun off, but this is not the explanation since it was deconsolidated as a discontinued operation. American Express Bank was comparatively small, but this accounted for much of the loans and deposits. Many other assets and liabilities also matched each other: insurance and investment liabilities moved with invested assets and the segregated assets and liabilities, as the name suggested, matched each other. As a purely analytical exercise, we can shrink the balance sheet by netting off these apparently matching items:

$ Millions	December 31, 1993
Receivables	16 142
Loans, net of deposits	3 665
Properties	1 976
Other	9 606
Total assets	31 389
Travelers checks	4 800
Debt, net of cash, investments, and reserves	4 588
Other	13 267
Shareholders' equity	8 734

This presents a fairer picture of the underlying leverage in the business.

The Lehman spin-off was completed in May 1994. Because of the 1993 accounting, it left most assets and liabilities unchanged. It did, however, take with it a portion of Amex's retained earnings, reducing shareholders' equity by $2.4 billion to $6.3 billion.

Consolidated statement of income, 1993

This was also suitably complex:

$ Millions	Year ended December 31, 1993
Commissions and fees	7 818
Interest and dividends	4 914
Premiums	702
Other	739
Total revenues	14 173
Overhead	(6 957)
Provisions	(3 107)
Interest	(1 783)
Lehman	(127)
Pre-tax income	2 199
Net income	1 478
EPS ($, continuing)	3.17

Aside from the Lehman effect, split out above, the company benefited from an after-tax gain of $433 million on its FDC shares. Adjusting the result for FDC and Lehman gives a net income of $1.2 billion and EPS of $2.51.

If the company's balance sheet was as leveraged as a bank's, it is instructive to see so little of the revenue coming from net interest income (most banking income is from this source). It is also worth noting that most of Amex's interest income was from a diversified and high-quality bond portfolio (like an insurer's) and little from risky loans (like a bank's). Perhaps not so apparent immediately was how little Amex's liabilities were costing. $85.4 billion non-equity liabilities led to $4.9 billion in interest cost and provisioning, or 5.7 per cent. As we know from Berkshire Hathaway's own progress, cheap liabilities can be as important as what your assets produce.

Sources of capital

Most of Amex's operations were cash generative. The large items on the balance sheet relating to the insurance/money management activities took in money well before it had to be returned (see GEICO case). The bank had more deposits than loans.

Amex had a strong source of capital in its image, summarized in its values and embodied in its brand.

Nevertheless, there were some $16 billion of charge-card receivables and $2 billion of properties to maintain and grow. Many analysts have noted that the travelers checks issued but not redeemed formed an effective "float." This was a good source of earnings, $4.8 billion at no cost, and some of these checks would *never* be presented, but this business was now a slow grower and could not support the asset gap identified. There were some free deposits produced by the bank but most of the work would have to be done by debt and retained earnings.

More figuratively, Amex had a strong source of capital in its image, summarized in its values and embodied in its brand. Golub had cut away the problems that threatened the company's strength and disposed of those businesses that did not promote the other values. Aside from the bank, which was a good effort to provide further services to wealthy individuals but had never quite come off, the core businesses generated good returns to capital and equity. This was possible in the crowded, disloyal financial services arena because Amex's customers were willing to pay a premium to be associated with the company. This was its true source of capital.

Return on equity

Post-Lehman, Amex's equity base had shrunk to $6.3 billion. Excluding the exceptional benefit from the sale of shares in FDC, continuing net income was $1.2 billion. ROE was, therefore, c.19 per cent. This makes intuitive sense in terms of the historic ROEs of the individual businesses we looked at (albeit before some corporate overhead). It is also comparable with the returns earned before the Shearson mess. No historic IP calculation is sensible because of the distortions the various capital-raising and disposal activities had wrought. Ongoing IP could very likely be at or above 19 per cent for the reasons given in the last section – the retained mix of activities were generally light on their capital needs or required about the same proportion as was then available.

> **Amex's customers were willing to pay a premium to be associated with the company.**

What was American Express worth?

One would have to be skeptical on intrinsic value at this stage. As good as the main businesses were, management had still not proven itself in the numbers. Historically, banks and insurers did not produce returns to equity of more than 10 per cent over a cycle. Amex was better than the average financial institution. Giving the new management benefit of the doubt and recognizing the continuing power of most of Amex's market positions, one could make a case for a sustainable IP and ROE of 19 per cent. Based on its continuing net income in 1993, which had grown somewhat in the first half of 1994, IV might be:

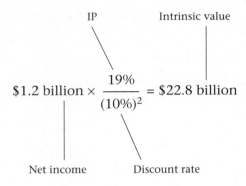

$$\text{\$1.2 billion} \times \frac{19\%}{(10\%)^2} = \text{\$22.8 billion}$$

WHAT BUFFETT DID

The $300 million matured in August 1994. The original terms called for this to be converted into 12.2 million shares subject to a maximum value of $414 million. The number of shares received was adjusted to 14 million because Berkshire had missed out on the Lehman distribution. The common traded at between $25.25 and $32 that quarter to give a value to Berkshire's stake of between $354 million and $448 million. Either way a nice capital gain in addition to the attractive dividend. Buffett has recently revealed that he was tempted to take the profit and sell the shares. Over a golf game with Frank Olson, CEO of Hertz, he was persuaded that Amex was fighting back against other card issuers and contained a number of strong franchises, particularly in the corporate market. Buffett decided that far from selling, he would buy and invested a further $1.1 billion in the common in the following few months. 1994 results were being announced during this time and showed good progression to $1.4 billion net, a 17 per cent increase. Based on that number IV would have risen to $26.6 billion.

Berkshire's new purchases were at an average of $30.80 per share, pricing the whole business at $15.7 billion. This gave a margin of safety based on the 1994 IV calculation of 41 per cent.

WHAT HAPPENED NEXT

Harvey Golub and his team fulfilled all their promise. Concentrating fully on the remaining businesses there was a clear, public identification of key driver, EPS growth and ROE targets. At TRS the emphasis was on increasing card membership, loyalty, and spending per card. Total cards in force increased 17 per cent compared to 1990, and total billing 87 per cent. The Financial Advisors business took full advantage of growing demand, stoked by demographic trends and the roaring bull markets. Assets owned or managed grew four times in seven years and earnings growth continued along its familiar and impressive 20 per cent p.a. path. The bank and travelers checks continued to go nowhere.

Underlying this performance was a rigid grasp on costs, which hardly now seemed to grow each year and much new product development, particularly the provision of new services to private and corporate cardmembers. The card market share started to grow for the first time in many years and there was a vigorous attack on Visa's grasp of banks as potential co-issuers.

Overall, net income in 1997 was $2 billion and EPS $4.2, recent growth of 13 per cent and 16 per cent p.a. respectively. As this implies there had been regular share repurchasing in modest amounts, stepping up in recent years. ROE had started to climb from 19–20 per cent to 22 per cent.

By the end of 1997, the share price was $89 and Berkshire Hathaway's $1.4 billion investment was worth $4.4 billion. Excluding dividends, this represented a remarkable c.39 per cent p.a. compounded appreciation since the 1994 decision.

EXERCISES

We saw that travelers checks provided a float to the company. Imagine that Amex's customers were less trusting and preferred depositing their money at a larger institution. However, Amex was able to produce the same profit from selling and redeeming checks.

1 Shareholders' equity became $6.3 billion after spinning off Lehman in 1999. What would it have been without the float?

2 What was the new ROE?

3 What was Intrinsic Value?

4 How would this have affected the 1994 investment decision?

Further questions for discussion

5 Strictly speaking, the loss of the float worth $4.8 billion should not affect the value of the company by more than that amount. Can you think of reasons why the apparent effect is more?

6 We have assumed that losing the float would not change Amex's income statement. Why might it affect revenues and costs in practice?

13

The Coca-Cola Company

Berkshire Hathaway bought ordinary stock in The Coca-Cola Company in 1988, 1989, and 1994 for a total cost of $1299 million.

HISTORY

Coca-Cola was incorporated in 1892 to exploit the new cocaine-based soft drink formulated by Dr John Pemberton of Georgia in 1886. It sold syrup to bottlers and other distributors and by 1895 was already selling 76 244 gallons, enough to make ten million drinks. Although cocaine was removed as an ingredient in 1902, the formula still employed psychologically comforting quantities of sugar and caffeine. Its market continued to expand, led by one of the largest advertising campaigns of its time, spending $85 000 in 1900 and $1 000 000 in 1912. Overseas operations were started in the 1920s, and in 1932 the company qualified for inclusion in the Dow Jones Industrial Average. A national institution in the Second World War, in the succeeding decades Coke's name, logo, and bottle shape became global icons.

> Although cocaine was removed as an ingredient in 1902, the formula still employed psychologically comforting quantities of sugar and caffeine. Its market continued to expand, led by one of the largest advertising campaigns of its time, spending $85 000 in 1900 and $1 000 000 in 1912.

Cuban émigré, Roberto Goizueta, became company president in 1980. Although revenues had reached $4.6 billion and profits after tax

$400 million, the company's management and message were tired. In partnership with chief operating officer, Don Keough, Goizueta took on the rival Pepsi – which had steadily gained market share – with a new marketing zeal. It is ironic that this management team is notorious for what has been called the biggest blunder in American marketing history. In response to market research showing consumers preferred the taste of Pepsi, New Coke was launched in 1985. New Coke performed well in taste trials, but the public response was swift, fierce, and unequivocal. After an unprecedented popular campaign, including 40 000 letters of protest, Classic Coke was reintroduced.

> It is ironic that this management team is notorious for what has been called the biggest blunder in American marketing history. In response to market research showing consumers preferred the taste of Pepsi, New Coke was launched in 1985. New Coke performed well in taste trials, but the public response was swift, fierce, and unequivocal. After an unprecedented popular campaign, including 40 000 letters of protest, Classic Coke was reintroduced.

Already the world's most widely distributed product and most recognized brand, the furore over New Coke proved one thing: people loved Coca-Cola.

COCA-COLA IN 1988

By the time Warren Buffett got around to looking at the company, New Coke had been forgotten by the public. Operating income fell slightly in 1985 but grew strongly in 1986 (34 per cent) and 1987 (26 per cent). Substantially all of this profit was earned from selling soft-drink syrup, as it had been for a hundred years. The gaffe, though, would have enabled him to answer the first of the three value questions:

Does the company provide value to its customers?

Coke's relationship with its consumers went beyond any other company's. Although only buying flavoured sugar-water, Coke drinkers were clearly at some level dependent on the drink. In 1987, the average American drank 274 servings of company products: the average Coke drinker probably drank more than one Coke per day every day.

Does the management provide value to the company?

The Goizueta-Keough team weathered the storm over New Coke and continued to grow the core soft-drinks business. Other business divisions were in related areas especially fruit juices. Significant capital expenditure was discretionary and tended to involve the acquisition of minority stakes in bottlers who remained key distributors. The most puzzling acquisition was of Columbia, a media business, for $750 million in 1984. Coca-

> In 1987, the average American drank 274 servings of company products: the average Coke drinker probably drank more than one Coke per day every day.

Cola was an important commissioner of commercials, but otherwise offered no obvious synergies. The business was well-managed though and a stock swap with Tri-Star took Columbia off-balance sheet while returning cash to shareholders. Crucially, management had principally focused on soft drinks while Pepsi had become increasingly diverted by its substantial snack-food and restaurant businesses.

Does the company provide value to its shareholders?

$100 invested in Coca-Cola ordinary stock at the end of 1982 would have been worth $270 with dividends reinvested at the end of 1987, giving 22 per cent p.a. compound growth. This compares with 13 per cent p.a. for the five previous years, that is, roughly the pre-Goizueta era. Management used a system that explicitly reinvested generated cashflow by reference to likely return on investment. And the company had started repurchasing its own stock in 1984.

A personal connection

- *Warren Buffett's personal connection with Coke starts with his first recorded business venture at the age of six! On vacation with his parents, he bought six bottles for 25 cents and sold them to neighboring vacationers for five cents apiece.*
- *He is a Cherry Coke addict, drinking an estimated five bottles a day.*
- *He was once a neighbor of Don Keough in Omaha. Keough is credited with converting Buffett from his long-standing preference for Pepsi in 1985.*

SOURCES OF INFORMATION

In 1988 Coke had been a familiar product for well over half a century. Although countless independent financial analyses and marketing studies were available, all of the key information Buffett needed was in the company's annual report. Apart from the normal financial measurements the report stated the following:

- Coca-Cola was "first and foremost a marketer of soft drinks"; 95 per cent of operating income came from this source;
- Soft drinks were characterized by "rapid volume growth, high margins, strong cashflow, low capital requirements and high return on investment." In Buffett's terms, this was a company facing an industry tailwind; and an ability to extract high amounts of cash relative to low reinvestment while growing profits was a very attractive combination;
- The soft-drinks business was the largest in the world. The company claimed the best distribution systems and the best brands while producing and facilitating bottling at the lowest costs in most of its 155 national markets;
- Buffett later wrote that apart from management's unusual blend of marketing and financial skills what most attracted him to the company was the realization that "sales overseas [were] virtually exploding".

Soft-Drinks Sales $m, to December	Domestic	International	International growth (%)
1985	1865	2677	
1986	2016	3629	36
1987	2120	4109	13

Most provocative would have been a table of the relative consumption of Coke and other company soft drinks in selected countries (these are actually adjusted figures from the 1988 report where the figures are clearer):

Country	Per capita consumption (8-ounce servings p.a.)
USA	277
Mexico	197
Australia	155
Norway	161
Canada	163
Germany	143
Argentina	155
Spain	103
Colombia	107
Philippines	79
Brazil	90
Italy	68
Great Britain	66
Korea	44
Japan	47
France	27
Thailand	25
Taiwan	17
Indonesia	3
China	0.3

To estimate roughly Coke's potential we can try a thought experiment. There are 250 million people in the USA and 4750 million elsewhere on the planet. Allowing for regional taste differences, strong local competition, political barriers, and so on, it is conceivable that Coca-Cola could over ten years increase non-US per capita consumption of its products to, say, half the US level. The 1987 international turnover of $4109 million would become $20 140 million at constant prices:

$$\frac{4750 \text{ million people}}{250 \text{ million people}} \times \begin{array}{l} 1987 \text{ US soft-drinks sales of} \\ \$2120m \times 50\% = \$20\ 140m \end{array}$$

In 1987 the international soft-drinks operating margin was 27 per cent. Allowing no economies of scale, but assuming all growth was internally financed, gives projected pre-tax profits of $5438m or income net of tax of, say, $3533m (at the company's then total tax rate). The long treasury yielded 9 per cent in 1987. If Coca-Cola could increase its product price each year at the then prevailing 3 per cent inflation rate we might discount the projected net income back at 6 per cent p.a. The present value of $3533m in ten years is $1973m, roughly tripling the company's 1987 net income.

> To estimate roughly Coke's potential we can try a thought experiment. There are 250 million people in the USA and 4750 million elsewhere on the planet. Allowing for regional taste differences, strong local competition, political barriers, and so on, it is conceivable that Coca-Cola could over ten years increase non-US per capita consumption of its products to, say, half the US level.

No one can predict the future with this kind of accuracy, but these are the kinds of assumptions that Buffett may have made when reading the annual report.

QUESTIONS TO TEST YOUR UNDERSTANDING

Do you understand why people buy the product?

Coke sold because it satisfied many millions of people's tastes. Methods of preparing, bottling, transporting and selling Coke had changed in its 100 years of history, but it was in essence doing the same thing it had always done. No special technological skill or even patented recipe guaranteed its future success. Anyone could understand that its appeal would continue.

How would the industry change in the next ten years?

Demand for Coke and Coca-Cola's other soft drinks was growing steadily as both the number of drinkers and the number of drinks they each bought grew. There were challenges from diet drinks and bottled water but the company had usually responded well, Diet Coke being the obvious example. The historic growth of Coke in the USA seemed a reasonable template for international expansion. While local economic conditions, tastes, and regulatory factors would vary, the company had shown its ability to market globally for 60 years. Also likely to continue was the ability of American brands, such as Mickey Mouse and the Big Mac, to symbolize freedom (particularly the freedom to consume) in a growing number of democratizing nation-states united by popular culture.

Are you comfortable with the management?

The Goizueta-Keough team had given a new edge to Coca-Cola's marketing and distribution systems. They were also careful only to invest cash where it could produce high incremental returns. Where this was no longer possible they returned excess cash to stockholders via dividends and stock repurchases. They were also committed to being the lowest-cost producer in the industry. If the stock market had closed Buffett could have rested easy.

Are there substitutes?

Coke competed with other soft drinks, non-carbonated drinks, bottled water, hot drinks, and tap water. Such an enormous and heterogenous market is practically impossible to measure. However, the soft-drinks market itself was growing more rapidly than any other type of beverage, and Coca-Cola dominated international soft drinks. Excluding the Soviet Union and China, Coca-Cola's international market share was 44 per cent, more than double its closest competitor. As significant, Coke was by a large measure the most recognized brand in the world, its manufacturing (including bottling) was the most efficient in the market and it had the widest distribution of any consumer product in the world. These all provided powerful and practically unbreakable barriers to entry into its growing share of the soft-drinks market. And while $900m in net profits might nevertheless sound like a powerful inducement to a new entrant, this was earned by selling the equivalent of over 191 billion drinks per year, a profit of under half a cent a time. This also provided effective protection against generic (or "no-name") producers.

FINANCIAL ANALYSIS

Given this combination of favorable circumstances, how had Coca-Cola's management fared until 1987? The annual report to December 31, 1987 included a summary of results for the previous 11 years.

$m	1987	1986	1985	1984	1983	1982	1981	1980	1979	1978	1977
Revenues	7558	6977	5879	5442	5056	4760	4836	4640	3895	3423	2753
Gross profit	4025	3523	2970	2704	2476	2288	2161	2046	1794	1569	1222
Operating income	1360	1077	807	849	828	773	720	680	644	602	528
Pre-tax income	1410	1208	992	982	927	873	771	707	691	635	561
Net income	916	798	678	622	553	494	432	394	386	351	310
Shares outstanding	377	387	393	396	408	390	372	372	372	372	369
EPS ($)	2.43	2.06	1.73	1.57	1.36	1.27	1.16	1.06	1.04	0.94	0.84

(Note: we have excluded exceptional items and adjusted tax accordingly.) Several facts jump out at once. Revenues had grown an impressive 2.75 times in ten years (or 10.6 per cent p.a.) but operating income before provisions had only grown 2.58 times. Given what we believe about the management team this relative laxity over general expenses would have been one of their main targets. And indeed, in the five years to 1987 the growth in operating income had accelerated to 12 per cent p.a. The per share data also falls into two periods – 1977–82 8.6 per cent p.a.; 1982–87 13.9 per cent p.a. It is not at all coincidental that the number of shares in issue rose in the first period as acquisitions were made and fell by almost the same amount in the second period as stock was repurchased. Let's look in more detail at the balance sheet now.

Consolidated balance sheets

The results for 1986 and 1985 had been restated. Two important financial maneuvers underlie this. First, the anomalous investment in Columbia, a media business, went part of the way to being disposed. It was merged with the similar Tri-Star studios and a significant stake was granted to Coca-Cola's shareholders as a one-time dividend. This not only took the now 49 per cent owned company off-balance sheet, it returned $335 million (albeit in the form of Columbia stock) to shareholders rather than remaining and burning a hole in management's pocket. Secondly, in 1986 the company's stake in Coca-Cola Enterprises Inc., the largest domestic bottler, had also been reduced to 49 per cent and taken off-balance sheet. Again this pointed up management's desire to focus Coca-Cola on what it did best – marketing not manufacturing. And as we shall see it had very positive effects on capital utilization.

We can get a handle on the 1987 balance sheet by shrinking it to its essentials (Figure 13.1).

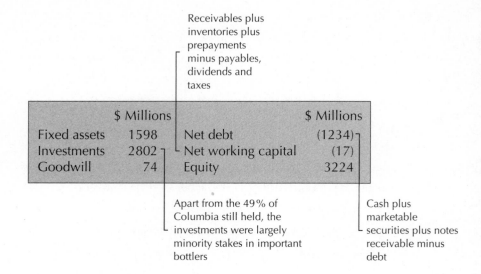

Figure 13.1
Coca-Cola: simplified balance sheet, 1987

The most remarkable thing about this balance sheet is its absolute size. For a business selling over $7 billion of a manufactured product in a year it has very little by way of current or long-term assets. Also captured by the above summary is the non-existent net working capital. Another way of looking at this is that the company was able to use its suppliers, deferred tax payments and the like to finance *all* of its working assets, such as inventories and amounts owed by customers. No reliance on debt and no use of shareholders' funds.

Consolidated statements of income

We have already learned that substantially all of the company's operating income was generated from soft drinks. A note gives the geographical breakdown for all products:

Note 17. Operations in geographic areas (condensed)

$ Millions – excludes provisions	USA	Latin America	Europe and Africa	Pacific and Canada	Corporate	Total
1985						
Revenues	3147	452	1241	1028	11	5879
Operating income	334	91	294	229	-141	807
1986						
Revenues	3278	556	1629	1502	12	6977
Operating income	409	141	400	352	-225	1077
1987						
Revenues	3459	558	1710	1917	15	7658
Operating income	421	153	508	453	-175	1360

This note not only reflects the continuing domestic growth in what one might have imagined was a mature market but terrific recent growth overseas, particularly in the Pacific – Japan is described as the company's top soft-drink profits contributor. And profit margins internationally were well over double what was being achieved in the home market.

Returning to the income statements we note briefly that very little interest is being paid net – the ratio of operating income before provisions to net interest is a comfortable 18.9 times. Equity income is the company's share of the net income of Columbia and the bottling companies in which it held minority stakes.

Cashflow

We can usefully condense these statements as follows:

$ Millions	1987	1986	1985
Stated net income	916	934	678
Exceptional income	–4	–195	54
Depreciation and amortization	154	155	133
Other	17	71	–62
Working capital	273	–69	–48
Capital expenditure	–300	–346	–384
Net investment	–564	–526	386
Dividends	–422	–403	–389
Net stock purchases	–564	–59	–186
Cash generated	–494	–438	182

Since the net change in investments is accounted for either by changes in marketable securities or entirely discretionary purchases of minority stakes in bottlers we can for our purposes ignore the "Net investment" line. The summary cashflow then demonstrates two points – how little working capital and fixed capital investment is needed to support the rapid income growth; and management's determination to return as much cash as possible to shareholders without reliance on gearing. All free cash flow is being returned to shareholders.

Owner earnings

Even though operating income had grown 69 per cent in the past two years, investment in the net tangible assets necessary to run the core business (that is, excluding bottler investment) were minimal in the case of working capital and about double depreciation for capital expenditure, fully explainable by income growth (the ratio of capital expenditure to net fixed assets is about the same as the income growth rate). It is quite likely that if there were no unit volume growth, owner earnings would equal or exceed stated profits. It is not necessary to estimate the difference, only to recognize the implications – growing or static, Coca-Cola would throw off cash.

Sources of capital

From a shareholders' equity base of $3.2 billion together with net debt of $700m the company generated revenues of $7.7 billion and net income of $900m. Since net working capital was minimal, the raw numbers suggest the company was making an excellent return on some non-controlled bottlers, a film studio and the syrup factories – an absurd idea. In reality Coca-Cola controlled some valuable assets not reflected on its balance sheet. We have already mentioned its brand, distribution system, and low-cost production. All of these generated large amounts of economic goodwill and were difficult to replicate.

> Since net working capital was minimal, the raw numbers suggest the company was making an excellent return on some non-controlled bottlers, a film studio and the syrup factories – an absurd idea. In reality Coca-Cola controlled some valuable assets not reflected on its balance sheet.

The unusual hidden asset was the relationship with bottlers. Why was $7.7 billion of revenue possible with only $1.6 billion of fixed assets and $800m of stock? Because the most capital-intensive part of the production process – the bottling – was largely owned and funded by third parties. Management reckoned that while bottling was important, it did not add much value to shareholders – it was capital intensive, open to competition and non-branded. This is of course arguable and the company itself hedged its bets by tying up over $1 billion in "affiliated" bottling investments in companies with which it wished a close relationship, but if you had the choice between investing in developing the Coke brand or its bottling plants, which would you choose? This might in practice depend on the strength of the bottling contract but over time the power is clearly with the owner of the brand not the bottles. If ownership of either were available at a reasonable price one would go for the former. (It should be noted that the final link in the distribution chain, retailing soft drinks in stores, restaurants, and the like, is even more capital-intensive and Coca-Cola was not in those businesses either.)

Return on equity

This was the ten-year record:

Millions	Net income (adjusted for exceptionals)	Average number of shares	Net debt/ (cash)	Shareholders' equity	Return on average equity (%)
Year					
1978	360	372	(256)	1740	21.7
1979	391	372	(23)	1919	21.4
1980	401	372	(22)	2075	20.1
1981	442	372	(117)	2271	20.3
1982	488	390	(239)	2779	19.3
1983	552	408	(39)	2921	19.4
1984	616	396	495	2778	21.6
1985	645	393	304	2979	22.4
1986	786	387	741	3515	24.2
1987	916	377	1234	3224	27.1

The company started repurchasing stock in 1984 and had by year-end 1987 spent $1.3 billion. In 1987 alone it had paid $605m for this purpose, more than its retained earnings. Again we can distinguish between the former and latter five-year periods. A creditable but flat return on equity of c.20 per cent on an ever higher equity base derived from retained earnings and share issues contrasts with accelerating income growth, stock repurchases and a rapidly growing ROE. (And although the increase in net debt looks alarming one should consider:

interest cover was very healthy at 18.9 times; net debt could have been repaid from just over one year's earnings; an adjusted return measure comparing earnings before net interest of, say, $1014m to equity plus net debt of $4458m still shows an impressive 22.7 per cent; and, in any case, the bulk of the recent increase in indebtedness was temporary and connected to the Columbia transaction.)

What was Coca-Cola worth?

We have seen that back-of-envelope projections based on international growth produced fancy profits numbers. What would a reasonable person have estimated the company's intrinsic value was in 1988? Having amply passed the qualitative tests we must consider recent historic financial performance. For the financial year-end of December 1987, net income before exceptionals was just over $900m. Buffett started buying in the summer when 1988 net income per share growth of at least 15 per cent could have been predicted; taking into account that only half the year was achieved, let's assume growth of only 7 per cent to give a base income of $980m. Goodwill amortization was immaterial. As suggested above, owner earnings were at least equal to net income – if unit volume had remained static, capital expenditure would have been unlikely to exceed depreciation and working capital may well have become cash positive. Return on average shareholders' equity was 27 per cent and growing. The dollar increase in net income from 1986 to 1987 was c.$130m and for 1988 would be about the same. Meanwhile, the annual retention in shareholders' equity was tricky to reckon. The combined effect of stock repurchases, the cash dividend and the special dividend in kind spinning off Columbia had led to a net reduction in equity in 1987. Adding back the special dividend leaves equity unchanged in the year. This was very creditable but not representative. We have seen that capital expenditure tended to exceed depreciation at least twice and that this was the only necessary investment underpinning growth (working capital was self-financing). The average net investment was $200m p.a. The growth in equity averaged 9 per cent between 1980 and 1986 or $290m now (9 per cent of the closing equity for 1987) and this figure also takes into account other investment activity. Coca-Cola's incremental return on equity was, therefore, around 45 per cent ($130m incremental income/$290m incremental equity).

Was 45 per cent a reasonable target for sustainable return on equity? Certainly, given the company's history, prospects and barriers to entry. At the currently achieved growth and retention rates it would probably achieve 45 per cent within four years. However, knowing Buffet's conservatism we would judge he made his purchase assuming 27 per cent was at the least a sustainable rate. Our measure of intrinsic value would be: $980m owner earnings × (27% sustainable ROE/(10% discount rate)^2) = $26 460m or $71.1 per share; there were 372 million shares outstanding at the end of 1987.

WHAT BUFFETT DID

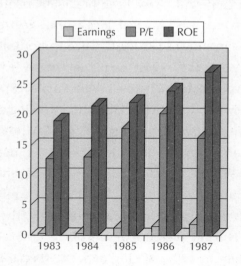

Figure 13.2
Earnings and value 1983–87

In the summer of 1988 Berkshire Hathaway started buying stock, ending the year with 14 172 500 shares at an average price of $41.81 for a total cost of $592.54m. Earnings per share in 1987 had been $2.42. The first two quarters of 1988's results implied a c.16 per cent increase for 1988 or $2.81 per share. Buffett was, therefore, paying between 14.9 and 17.3 times earnings.

1988 was in fact another vintage year for Coca-Cola. Revenues and operating income were 8.9 per cent and 17.5 per cent higher respectively after significant volume gains in the international soft-drinks business. Stated earnings per share ended up 18 per cent higher at $2.85 and were probably closer to $2.95 before exceptionals. Buffett's true p/e on his initial purchases was, therefore, close to 14. Coca-Cola spent $759m repurchasing its stock in 1988, again using all its generated cashflow on this and dividends, so that ordinary shareholders' equity fell to $3,045m and ROE rose to a startling 34.5 per cent.

Berkshire Hathaway invested a further $491m for 9 177 500 shares at an average of $53.5 per share in 1989. Again, the first half results implied a bumper year with earnings per share up 22 per cent, giving predicted earnings of $3.49. The p/e for the 1989 purchases was, therefore, between 15.3 and 18.1.

What happened next

Berkshire did in fact make one more purchase of Coke stock in 1994. At an average cost of $166.7 per share it spent a further $275m. Although a relatively small addition to a stake then worth over $4 billion, it is an intriguing one since the prevailing p/e was one of the highest Buffett had paid to date. To give perspective let's bring the story up to date.

Coca-Cola continued to grow. Between 1987 and 1995 revenues, continuing net income and continuing net income per share grew 11.3 per cent, 15.6 per cent, and 19.5 per cent p.a. respectively. The Columbia stake was sold at a substantial profit in 1989 and the company continued to take minority stakes in bottlers to help them improve their efficiency. A comparison between the two balance sheets is instructive.

Balance sheets, 1987–95

$ Millions	1987	1995		1987	1995
Fixed assets	1598	4336	Net debt	(1234)	(1503)
Investments	2802	2714	Net working capital	(17)	(133)
Goodwill	74	944	Other	0	(966)
			Equity	3224	5392

As one would have expected from our analysis of the 1987 accounts, net capital expenditure has continued to grow, although in fact at a slightly slower rate than net income (13.3 per cent p.a.). Taking into account the Columbia divestiture and the accumulated goodwill, investment in affiliates is somewhat larger but still modest compared to the size of earnings. Noteworthy are the working capital and debt entries which have barely changed in eight years. Incremental equity totaled $2.2 billion in a period in which income had grown by $2 billion – a year.

> The thought experiment we looked at earlier, growing the international business consistently and rapidly with relatively little incremental equity, had come to pass and growth continued to accelerate.

Net income was in fact almost $3 billion in 1995. Virtually 100 per cent of income derived from selling drinks, 82 per cent from outside the USA, although the domestic market continued to grow. The company had repurchased 459 million shares for a total of $8.8 billion by year-end and return on average equity was a mighty 55 per cent.

By the end of 1995 Berkshire Hathaway's stake had grown from a cost of $1.3 billion to a value of $7.4 billion. It had earned c.$400 million in cash dividends. And taking into account share repurchases it now owned 8 per cent of the company. It is important to appreciate that although between 1987 and 1995 the share price had increased 7.8 times, earnings per share had increased an impressive but lower 4.2 times. The stock market had almost doubled the p/e ratio at which shares could be bought:

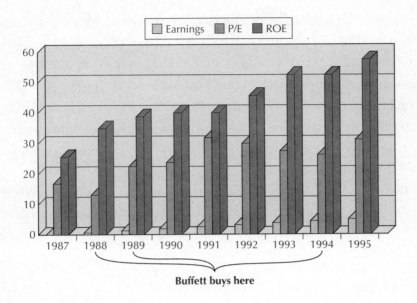

Buffett buys here

Figure 13.3
Earnings and value 1987–95

Buying in 1994 Buffett had been willing to pay an historic p/e of 24.8 on 1993 earnings. The 1994 first-half results would have been enough to convince him that earnings would grow by over 20 per cent that year bringing the effective p/e to 20.7. This was still a higher ratio than he had traditionally paid for common stocks and some way above the prospective p/e of 15 he had paid earlier. There are two likely explanations. First, he knew and was comfortable with the company and its management by now. The thought experiment we looked at earlier, growing the international business consistently and rapidly with relatively little incremental equity, had come to pass and growth continued to accelerate. With return on equity just

> Prize for the most optimistic goal though must go to the following question and answer in the 1995 report: "What's our most underdeveloped market? The human body. People can do without most things for an entire day. But every day, every one of the 5.7 billion people on this planet must consume roughly 64 ounces of fluid to live. We currently account for less than 2 of those ounces."

over 50 per cent and set to grow further a p/e of 20 still gave a good margin of safety. (1993 net income $2.2 billion × (50% ROE/(10% discount rate)^2) = $110 billion or $262 per share. There had been a number of share splits, but Buffett paid the equivalent of $167 per share.

Considerable portions of the Coca-Cola annual report were dedicated to showing that the best growth was yet to come. Prize for the most optimistic goal though must go to the following question and answer in the 1995 report: "What's our most underdeveloped market? The human body. People can do without most things for an entire day. But every day, every one of the 5.7 billion people on this planet must consume roughly 64 ounces of fluid to live. We currently account for less than 2 of those ounces."

By the end of 1997 net income had grown to $4.1 billion. Berkshire's stake was worth $13.3 billion, excluding cash dividends received.

EXERCISES

How would Coca-Cola's value be affected if it were also responsible for bottling and distribution?

1 Consider the 1985–87 period. Assume that the new activities require as much equity again but only generate a return of 10 per cent. Using the same rate of income growth, recalculate ROE.

2 Estimate Intrinsic Value.

3 How would this have affected your decision to invest in 1988? At what price might you have invested?

Further questions for discussion

4 What would be the effect on ROE/IP if income and equity continue to grow at the annualized rates assumed in the above questions?

5 How would ROE/IP and intrinsic value be altered if the rate of income growth slows to reflect the lower returns in bottling?

GEICO

Berkshire Hathaway bought ordinary and convertible preference shares equaling 33.3 per cent of GEICO Corporation in 1976, 1979, and 1980, at a total cost of $47.1 million. GEICO repurchased its own stock over the following 20 years such that Berkshire owned about 51 per cent. At the beginning of 1996, Berkshire paid $2.3 billion for the remaining 49 per cent of GEICO.

HISTORY

GEICO stands for Government Employees Insurance Company. For most of its life it has specialized in providing automobile insurance to low-risk groups such as government employees, military personnel, and older people. It was founded by a Texas insurance accountant, Leo Goodwin, in 1936 with $100 000 in capital. In 1937, he and his wife, Lillian, moved to Washington to be closer to their target customers. From the beginning they had two advantages which have remained with GEICO. By aiming at safer drivers only, they were creaming off the better risk from less discriminating insurers. They also decided to sell direct to the public, principally by mail. Almost all personal insurance was sold through

> GEICO stands for Government Employees Insurance Company. For most of its life it has specialized in providing automobile insurance to low-risk groups such as government employees, military personnel, and older people.

agents, adding considerably to the industry's cost base. GEICO's premium income was around $1.5 million per annum by 1945.

A majority stake was sold to Ben Graham and his associates in 1948 and Graham became chairman. The business continued to identify and target low-risk groups throughout the USA, and profits grew through the 1950s and 1960s as the benefits of low costs were passed back to customers as low prices.

In the early 1970s, under new management, GEICO started to accept higher risk auto and non-automobile customers. The book grew rapidly as did central expenses. Unhappily management had been under-reserving for these higher-risk policies. The high inflation of this period forced up the cost of automotive repairs and property rein- statement. At the end of 1975 the board received an independent actuarial report stating that the business needed an urgent injection of at least $50 million to remain solvent. The stock had fallen from $60 to $40; the prospect of losing everything now drove it to $2. The chief executive left and the Washington, DC insurance superintendent threatened to shut down the business.

The personal connection

Buffett's love affair with GEICO was an offshoot of his hero worship of Ben Graham. As a 20-year-old student of Graham's, Buffett discovered that his teacher was chairman of GEICO and made an unannounced visit to the Washington HQ one Saturday in 1951. The office was closed but the only person working that day took Buffett in and spent several hours explaining GEICO's enduring competitive advantages. This was Lorimer Davidson who was to become chief executive in the 1960s. Back in 1951, Buffett bought $10 000 of the stock but was to sell out for a 50 per cent capital gain a year later.

GEICO IN 1976

GEICO in 1976 was a disaster. It declared a loss in 1975 of $126 million and would lose a further $26 million in 1976. A major step toward recovery was the hiring of Jack Byrne, a tough 43-year-old from Travelers, as the new CEO. He withdrew the business from two states that would not allow higher rates, repriced all new business, fired half the workforce and shut down a number of regional offices. The higher pricing and general disorder led to a haemorrhaging of policies in force, falling from 2.7 million to 1.5 million by the end of 1977. This was a turnaround, but it was still important to ask the three value questions.

Does the company provide value to its customers?

Buffett realized that beneath the rubble GEICO still possessed a valuable consumer franchise. Like American Express and its salad oil scandal in the 1960s a disaster at the corporate level did not really affect the perception of loyal customers. Although GEICO's customer base had nearly halved a lot of the lost business was company-induced – in unwelcoming states and higher-risk categories of drivers, for example. For core customers, safer drivers buying by mail, the company still provided cheaper insurance and good service. There had been high renewal rates (the per centage of existing policyholders offered renewals who accepted) and strong positive word-of-mouth which was likely to revive if the business were stable. Above all, GEICO's status as *the* low-cost car insurer was untouched. Insurance companies that had relied on brokers and sales forces in 1930s still relied on them. Even though direct response marketing was clearly cheaper, other insurers did not want to offend or cannibalize business from their existing distribution channels. It was not impossible for an existing insurer to enter the direct response market but they did not because they were institutionally managed and competed in traditional ways. Meanwhile GEICO's cost advantage was becoming stronger through economies of scale.

Does the management provide value to the company?

The existing management did not. Jack Byrne was untested. Buffett arranged to see Byrne and spent several hours interviewing him before taking any action. He confirmed what Buffett already suspected: the low-cost base was still in place. If the company could raise capital and placate its regulators a remarkable business might re-emerge. Buffett was also impressed by Jack Byrne. He was an insurance pro and had already done what was needed to start the turnaround. He had exited unprofitable policies and lines of business and cut back the company so that it could focus on its golden egg. Byrne had the measure of the problem and the guts to see through the solution.

Does the company provide value to its shareholders?

The company had almost gone bust and had already beggared a number of its shareholders, but like American Express in the 1960s and Wells Fargo in the 1980s, Buffett applied his own criteria to turnarounds if he understood the underlying business. Gillette, Coca-Cola, and Walt Disney had delivered consistently good operating returns, although their fortunes fluctuated on Wall Street. GEICO was close to bankruptcy.

SOURCES OF INFORMATION

For the initial investment in 1976, 1975 financial information would certainly not have been enough. Earnings were negative and the business was all but insolvent. Businesses like insurance, leasing, banking and oil and gas need some specialist knowledge because the lead time for establishing the true value of the assets or, in insurance's case, the liabilities is long. Each year an insurer must estimate the likely claims that will arise from that year's new policies and re-estimate previous years' provisions in light of experience. Investors are more than usually at the mercy of insiders. Some insurers, particularly those managed by actuaries, are so conservative in their accounting that they provide unusually favorable opportunities to invest. This was not the problem at GEICO.

There is more on insurance in Chapter 2. Suffice to say that insurance was already Berkshire's biggest business in 1976 and Buffett knew the industry well. He used two measures to establish the attractiveness of an insurance company. The combined ratio compares the annual costs to annual revenues:

$$\text{Combined ratio} = \frac{\text{Estimated losses plus expenses} \times 100}{\text{Premiums earned}}$$

Because insurers earn a return from the float – the money they hold between taking in premiums and paying out claims plus their own capital – they are often content to suffer a combined ratio above 100, an underwriting loss. GEICO had historically averaged below 100 because of its low costs, making an underwriting profit. The average insurer in the early 1970s had roughly double the overhead expense of GEICO as a per centage of premiums earned.

The other measure Buffett applied was a comparison of underwriting cost or profit to float:

Insurance profit = Underwriting cost + (Float × Discount rate)

Even simple insurance companies contain three businesses. The underwriting business provides a profit or loss, shown by the combined ratio. If there is an underwriting loss it can still be compensated for by the investment income produced by the float. The Insurance Profit measure shows what this would be if the float were simply invested at a notional discount rate – Buffett uses the long treasury rate for the current year. The third business is investment. A good investment manager will outperform the discount rate:

Investment profit = Achieved rate of return × Float

At this time GEICO had no particular investment advantage. It did, though, have considerable attractions demonstrated by its historic Combined Ratio and Insurance Profit performance. To maintain cost advantage it passed back to its customers a part of its low expenses as low pricing. Even while maintaining and extending its cost leadership it had been able to achieve a combined ratio of below 97. In its reduced state GEICO still had premium income of $575 million and some $600 million of investments.

QUESTIONS TO TEST YOUR UNDERSTANDING

Do you understand why people buy the product?

It was a legal requirement to hold car insurance and more people than ever were driving. GEICO had been adept at identifying low-risk groups, who also turned out to be loyal in their renewals.

How would the industry change in the next ten years?

The industry was conservative. Apart from technology to store data little had changed in decades. Insurance was also highly regulated and few would have predicted major industry change.

Are you comfortable with the management?

We are reliant on Buffett's assessment of Byrne in this case. We have seen that he believed Byrne already had GEICO's problems in hand. An important management skill in underwriting insurance is discipline. Writing business is analogous to investing. Nobody compels you to take particular risks. Most insurance companies do not drastically alter their appetite for types of risk at different times. In the real world conditions change. Juries increase damages or there is a recession; most insurers attempt to catch up "over the cycle". And, like bankers, insurers move in packs. If conditions happen to be good in one market, every insurance company with an eye out will dive in until prices are driven down. Once in that market the companies continue to write business at much the same rate, waiting for an upturn. A good insurer, a disciplined insurer, will only write policies he or she believes will be profitable, and will reduce capacity if pricing is forced down. Buffett believed that Byrne was decisive and able to identify with the stockholders, as well as staff and customers.

Are there substitutes?

The industry was very competitive. There was little that one company could do to differentiate its service or products over time. Buffett wrote about his own insurance operations in 1977 that pricing was transparent and no branding, history, or government protection would provide cover. He emphasized management as the key to success. Repeatedly he has publicly judged his insurance managers in two ways – how disciplined their underwriting is, and to what combined ratio this translates. Buffett and Munger handle the investment side themselves. GEICO's discipline had been poor but Buffett believed that Byrne would restore the old selectivity. What was difficult for competitors to reproduce was cost leadership. The question analysts had always asked was why other insurance companies let GEICO get away with it. It was possible that another company would enter the market but few had. Their dedication to salespeople and brokers and their regard for conventional competitors blinded them to GEICO's creeping advantage. It was a top-twenty insurer by 1975.

> Buffett prefers the lowest-cost supplier. A common image he used was that of a moat around a business. GEICO had built a moat and had used its growing size to widen and deepen it.

As we saw in Chapter 5, in industries like retailing and banking, where competitive advantage through differentiation is difficult to sustain, Buffett prefers the lowest-cost supplier. A common image he used was that of a moat around a business. GEICO had built a moat and had used its growing size to widen and deepen it. Its essential economic advantage had not been fatally damaged by losses in other sectors. The moat endured.

FINANCIAL ANALYSIS

Investing in a turnaround required good industry knowledge, belief in management, evidence that the underlying economics were intact and some courage. Financial analysis of recent performance was not encouraging. What could be constructed was a rough model of what the remaining assets and liabilities of GEICO could hope to produce if recapitalized and managed tightly.

The underlying position in 1975–6 was somewhat murky because of one-off costs, the ongoing cost-reduction exercise and the current and historic reserving errors. In the 1976 balance sheet, assets were over

$900 million, of which c.$600 million were in investments. $575 million of premium income was earned that year producing a loss of $26 million.

Balance sheet, 1976

1976	$ Million
Premiums earned	575.4
Net investment income	38.1
Total revenue	613.5
Total benefits and expenses	639.9
Operating earnings	(26.4)
Investment gains[1]	0.1
Net income[2]	(26.3)

Notes

1. Investment gains were capital gains in the investment portfolio and, like Berkshire's, were periodic and unpredictable in size. GEICO held few equities or other securities without a set maturity and this element of profit was likely to remain small.
2. Because of the loss no tax was payable.

Sources of capital

Like many other Berkshire investments, GEICO had an unusual source of cheap capital, its float. Berkshire knew all about this since it had benefited from a cheap or free float since its purchase of National Indemnity in 1967. If GEICO could regain its accustomed combined ratio below 100, the entire float would effectively cost nothing. Any underwriting profit would be a bonus.

Return on equity

Given an underwriting profit, what could a reconstructed GEICO earn? Buffett had to assume that there would be further policyholder fallout. On the other hand he knew that price increases Byrne had already implemented would feed through into increased revenue per policy.

He would already have known the approximate premium level for 1976. However, he could only estimate how far premiums would fall. A safe assumption would have been a loss of one-third of what remained, from 2 million to 1.33 million policyholders, and premium income of $383 million, $420 million after price increases. A reduction in business would ultimately also decrease the float from $600 million to, say, $438 million (a pro rata reduction with the premium level).

Buffett would have been able to forecast earnings simply from this information. With a traditional combined ratio of about 97, the $420 million of premium income would have produced c.$13 million underwriting profit. The year-end yield on long-term treasuries was 8 per cent, so $438 million of float would have earned at least $35 million, to give total income before tax of $48 million. Even though GEICO had tax losses, Buffett was interested in the *sustainable* return to equity. Insurance tax is complex, with many exemptions, but a typical insurer with GEICO's profile might have paid 25 per cent income tax, leaving net income of $36 million.

> Like many other Berkshire investments, GEICO had an unusual source of cheap capital, its float.

There were 18 million ordinary shares outstanding at the end of 1975 and book value was around $54 million, with long-term debt owing of $48 million. GEICO was seeking to raise $76 million to shore up the balance sheet and had been rejected by a number of investment banks who thought the company unsaveable.

What was GEICO worth?

Many bankers, investors and regulators thought it was worth nothing. With a number of hefty assumptions we can conjure up a going concern value. If it could raise the $76 million, contain the remaining losses, preserve its licences and resurrect its franchise we estimated it might earn $36 million fully taxed. The new capital would more or less cancel out the cost of the existing debt. The new book value would be $130 million ($54 million existing plus $76 million new capital).

This would give a new ROE of:

$$\frac{\text{Net income}}{\text{Shareholders' equity}} : \frac{36}{130} = 28\%$$

This is a tendentious figure since the equity is the sum of a che-quered history – big losses artificially boost a one-year ROE (see Chapter 10). We cannot take an IP reading for lack of data. IP is not really appropriate in this industry anyway. Say premium income grows at 5 per cent annually, or $21 million in year one. At the assumed com-bined ratio incremental underwriting profit would be $630 000. If float grew proportionately the extra cash generated would be $21.9 million producing $1.75 million additional investment income at the 8 per cent assumed rate of return. This extra income after tax would be $1.79 million. It would be unnecessary to retain any of this income since the additional float is more than sufficient to satisfy any capital requirements. The general conclusion is that an insurer routinely pro-ducing a combined ratio below 100 will throw off cash and, apart from regulatory requirements, does not need incremental capital investment. As we saw in Chapter 2 this is why the industry has been so attractive to Berkshire Hathaway.

In the absence of suitable ROE or IP measures we can still make an intelligent estimate of new GEICO's intrinsic value. Since we are assuming that it would routinely make an underwriting profit its float would effectively come free. Deducting the 25 per cent tax payment due on annual investment income implies the $438 million float is worth $329 million in shareholders' hands. The $13 million under-writing profit is worth $10 million after tax. At a lowly multiple of 10 this adds $100 million to give a total value of $429 million. In con-ventional p/e terms this is just under 12 times the estimated ongoing profits, a rate under which many insurers were selling in private and public transactions at the time. Without being able to estimate IP or ROE we cannot justify precisely a higher figure. The cash-generative nature of the business and its underlying franchise suggest that these are conservative numbers.

WHAT BUFFETT DID

He made his first purchases even before the recapitalization. Straight after his meeting with Byrne he placed orders for 500 000 shares. Berkshire ultimately bought 1.3 million shares in that period for $4.1 million, or $3.18 per share. At this price the cost of the company and the margin of safety were:

$3.18 per share × 18 million shares = $57.2 million company cost. Since this was before the new $76 million was injected –

$$\text{Margin of safety} = \frac{\$429 \text{ million} - \$76 \text{ million} - \$57 \text{ million}}{\$429 \text{ million} - \$76 \text{ million}} = 84\%$$

Clearly the considerable risk inherent in a turnaround was balanced by the large upside. But Buffett and Munger have rejected hundreds of such opportunities. I am sure that as important as the numbers in their minds were the qualitative factors of management and competitive advantage.

With Berkshire Hathaway providing partial sub-underwriting, Salomon agreed to underwrite the $76 million which was structured as 7.8 million units of convertible preferred stock at $9.80 per unit. Each stock unit was entitled to a preferred dividend of $0.74 (7.5 per cent) and could be converted at any time into two ordinary shares, that is, an effective price of $4.90 per share.

GEICO now had 34 million common stock equivalents outstanding. The price for this round of financing was $4.90 per share. The new margin of safety was therefore:

$4.90 per share × 34 million shares = $167 million cost

$$\text{Margin of safety} = \frac{\$429 \text{ million} - \$167 \text{ million}}{\$429 \text{ million}} = 61\%$$

At this lower margin of safety, but for a rather better financed and, therefore, safer company, Berkshire took almost 2 million new units for $19.4 million. It now owned 25 per cent of the preferred issue and 16 per cent of the total common stock equivalents.

GEICO IN 1979 AND 1980

The business looked a lot healthier. Byrne continued to hold the company by the scruff of its neck and did everything he promised; 90 per cent of the business was now in traditional preferred automobile policies; 90 per cent of these clients renewed year-on-year. After a further dip in premium income, from $575 million to $463 million in 1977, there had been a dramatic recovery to $605 million in 1978. The actual number of policies in force had dropped slightly between 1977 and 1978, but the pricing had improved considerably. The combined ratio was as follows:

%	1978	1977	1976
Loss ratio	80.8	84.4	98.2
Expense ratio	14.9	14.8	12.4
Combined ratio	95.7	99.2	110.6

The jump in the expense ratio between 1976 and 1977 was almost wholly explicable by the drop in premiums. The real story was the drop in the loss ratio. The float meanwhile had moved above $1 billion. It had grown by two-thirds in two years, partly because premium volume had been maintained and partly because of retained earnings. Investment income had, therefore, hiked up as well, to $64 million. The historic losses meant no tax had to be paid yet but on a notionally fully taxed basis results would have been:

$ Millions	1978	1977	1976
Premiums earned	605	464	575
Net investment income	63	41	38
Other	2	1	–
Costs, including tax	(608)	(467)	(640)
Net income	62	38	(26)

N.B. This excludes investment portfolio capital gains and losses.

The company had made a small loss in 1976 as expected, and well within the capital available. Although the premium income had then dropped as expected, this was more than compensated for by higher pricing leading to a higher float/investment income and lower provisioning than anticipated in our forecast. The return to underwriting form in 1978 was the cherry on the cake and profits increased a further 50 per cent.

At the 1978 year-end, shareholders' equity was $223 million, giving an ROE on this figure of 28 per cent. There was no reason to suppose this figure would decline since income growth could be supported by additions to the float rather than retained earnings. There were certain regulations requiring retentions, but GEICO was not now at these limits. An intrinsic value calculation at 28 per cent would show:

$$\frac{28\%}{(10\%)^2} \times \$62 \text{ million} = \$1.7 \text{ billion}$$

Berkshire converted its preferred into common in 1979 and bought 462 000 more common for $4.8 million, or $10.30 per share. With the equivalent of 34 million shares still outstanding, this new purchase capitalized GEICO and implied a margin of safety as follows:

$$\$10.30 \text{ per share} \times 34 \text{ million} = \$350 \text{ million}$$

$$\text{Margin of safety} = \frac{\$1700 \text{ million} - \$350 \text{ million}}{\$1700 \text{ million}} = 79\%$$

Even though the share price had more than doubled since Berkshire's last purchase, the excellent profit performance combined with a more stable capital base would have given Buffett the comfort that an unmissable margin of safety had again appeared. All this at a time when the p/e that the market allowed was still only a miserable 5–6. You may feel that Berkshire's initial purchases would have been difficult to replicate, relying on too much inside access. An interesting conclusion from the last calculation is that you could have achieved the same margin of safety after the capital injection and turnaround as before.

At the operating level, 1979's results were mixed. Premiums grew c.5 per cent to $635 million, and the loss ratio improved almost two points to 79.1 per cent. More money was spent on direct mail and other central expenses, perhaps to counteract the slow growth. After a full tax charge, net income fell slightly to $60 million. Without one other important factor, though, net income would have grown proportionately with earned premiums: interest charged jumped from $4.2 million in 1978 to $10.2 million in 1979. Early in 1979 GEICO started repurchasing common and preferred shares. Taking advantage of its new creditworthiness, it issued $73.3 million 11 per cent debentures. With the cash it purchased $18.7 million face value of the preferred for $20.9 million and $50 million of common stock. At the end of 1979 only 25.2 million common stock equivalents were outstanding, a drop of 26 per cent. Excluding investment gains and losses and tax effects earnings per share increased 23 per cent to $2.14. Even net of retained earnings, shareholders' equity dropped from $223 million to $193 million. ROE increased from 28 per cent to 31 per cent, or 29 per cent on average equity over 1979.

Given the slightly reduced earnings and the higher ROE, it would be safe to assume an intrinsic value not much higher than the previous year's. What really impressed Buffett and Munger was Byrne's recognition that GEICO's surplus capital could best be invested by repurchasing its own capital. What were its alternatives? Its own operations were self-financing. It could have owned a higher float, at a pre-tax return of 10–11 per cent. Or it could have bought another business, possibly for a p/e of 10–15, or an earnings yield of 6–10 per cent. In buying its own shares it was investing in the business it knew best, where it had confidence value would grow – and, at a p/e of below 6, its initial return on investment was over 16 per cent.

The confirmed recovery of GEICO's franchise and the pro-shareholder actions of management persuaded Berkshire to invest a further $18.9 million in 1980. This bought 1.47 million of the common at $12.80 per share. The market "value" and margin of safety in 1980 were:

$$\$12.80 \times 25.2 \text{ million common share equivalents} =$$
$$\$323 \text{ million company cost}$$

$$\text{Margin of safety} = \frac{\$1700 \text{ million} - \$323 \text{ million}}{\$1700 \text{ million}} = 81\%$$

After further stock repurchases by GEICO in 1980, Berkshire Hathaway owned 33 per cent of the company by the year-end. It had invested \$47.1 million in total and was already showing over 100 per cent profit, excluding dividends. Buffett noted in his 1980 annual report that this \$47 million investment bought Berkshire \$20 million in earning power (one-third of GEICO's net income). The least you might pay for these earnings with good prospects might be \$200 million.

GEICO IN 1996

GEICO stuck to its knitting, more or less. There were some diversions into consumer finance, reinsurance, and other bywaters, but it concentrated on car drivers. In 1995 it earned \$2787 million from insurance premiums, 9.1 per cent p.a. compound growth since 1979. It was now the seventh largest auto insurer in the USA and still one of the best underwriters; in 1995 its combined ratio was 96.7 and it had bobbed around 97 through the 1980s and 1990s.

The float was now \$3 billion, but including shareholders' funds total investments were \$5 billion. Probably the most important change was in its "third business", how it invested its cash. Like many other insurers in the 1970s, GEICO had rather unthinkingly been happy to hold large amounts of medium- and long-term bonds. These were vulnerable to inflation and the hike in interest rates over that decade – they doubled – led to losses in many portfolios. While holding to maturity might have cleaned up the losses, in practice a large part of these holdings needed to be liquidated to meet claims and actual losses were realized.

> GEICO stuck to its knitting, more or less. There were some diversions into consumer finance, reinsurance, and other bywaters, but it concentrated on car drivers.

The best such a portfolio could aim for was to maintain its real value. GEICO had a better opportunity. If it kept its combined ratio below 100 it could reserve part of its float for the long term and turn to value investing.

Buffett was keen to convert management to the Graham method. He helped Jack Byrne recruit a new investment chief in 1979 called Lou Simpson and was soon giving talks on value principles to Simpson and other GEICO staff. The theme: how to get $1 by investing 50 cents. Simpson bought into this. GEICO kept a substantial portion of its portfolio in fixed-term securities for regulatory and practical reasons but it shortened the average life considerably: in 1980, 59 per cent matured over ten years, in 1995, 8 per cent. Lou Simpson, who had primary responsibility for equity investment, has been described by Buffett as the best investor in the property-casualty industry. Buffett has now named Simpson as his successor in managing Berkshire's quoted investments.

> Buffett was keen to convert management to the Graham method. He helped Jack Byrne recruit a new investment chief in 1979 called Lou Simpson and was soon giving talks on value principles to Simpson and other GEICO staff. The theme: how to get $1 by investing 50 cents.

What was GEICO worth in 1995?

The underwriting profit in 1995 was $92 million. The company was in the middle of getting out of a number of lines of business, particularly homeowners' insurance. As before, GEICO did best by coming back to its core market. It is possible, therefore, that this underwriting result, while still ahead of its peers, was lower than it could expect from automobile business alone. Net investment income was $227 million. After interest expense of $34 million and tax but before investment gains, net income was $235 million. The balance sheet consisted of the $5 billion in investments and $1 billion in other assets less $4 billion liabilities, primarily insurance reserves and a little debt. Shareholders' equity was $1.9 billion but that had been boosted in 1995 by a large unrealized investment gain. Underlying equity was closer to $1.5 billion. Even at this lower level ROE was only 16 per cent, good but not what we might have expected. The reason is the same as that underlying Berkshire's valuation in Chapter 2. With a substantial proportion of its portfolio tied up in relatively low-yielding bonds, investment income would appear low. Equally, the equity portion only reflected dividend income. As at Berkshire, the retained earnings of its investees were not reflected on the income statement, although they would ultimately turn up as capital gains. This kind of business gain is periodic and its effect difficult to capture.

We might approach valuation in a different way. GEICO's under-writing business made $92 million, say $69 million after tax. Let us assume that this part of the business was worth 15 times earnings of $1.035 billion. Since the combined ratio was routinely below 100 the investment side, including the float, came free. $5 billion can be mea-sured in many ways but it is safe enough to say that it is worth $5 billion (although this will depend on the tax status of the owner). So one guess of the intrinsic value is $6 billion. It is also possible to con-struct an estimate of ROE. If the $5 billion were all invested at the nominal discount rate of 10 per cent, net income would be:

Investment income   Underwriting   Tax
profit

$$[(\$5 \text{ billion} \times 10\%) + \$92 \text{ million}] \times 75\% = \$444 \text{ million}$$

$$\text{The ROE would be } \frac{444}{1500} = 30\%$$

$$\text{Intrinsic value would be } \frac{30\%}{(10\%)^2} \times \$444 \text{ million} = \$13.3 \text{ billion}$$

This seems high for a company which has so much of its net worth in liquid investments – surely the $6 billion is more appropriate? We should remember what the ROE calculation is telling us. GEICO may have had a $6 billion sum-of-the-parts value, but its ability to reemploy generated earnings and float in its business was still unrivalled by the competition. If it could continue to expand its business profitably at 10 per cent p.a. it would churn out ever larger underwriting profits and float. The $13.3 billion is realistic.

GEICO continued to repurchase its shares steadily until in 1996 Berkshire Hathaway owned just over 50 per cent of the company. At the beginning of 1996, Berkshire paid $2.3 billion for the half of GEICO it did not own.

$$\text{Margin of safety} = \frac{\$13.3 \text{ billion} - \$4.6 \text{ billion}}{\$13.3 \text{ billion}} = 65\%$$

Since Berkshire was paying less than the value of the $5 billion investment portfolio on its own, I think this is one acquisition that would have made Benjamin Graham smile.

EXERCISES

1 Give three reasons why a combined ratio of below 100 is commercially advantageous to a property-casualty insurer.

Further questions for discussion

2 How will the internet change GEICO's competitive environment?

3 What would be the very worst things that could happen to GEICO?

The Gillette Company

Berkshire Hathaway bought convertible preferred stock in The Gillette Company in 1989 for $600 million, converting into common stock in 1991.

HISTORY

Like many great enterprises, Gillette was founded on the force of one character, King C. Gillette. A salesman for an unrelated business, he had long been looking for a consumer product with which to establish his fortune. In 1895 he settled on the disposable razor blade, forming the American Safety Razor Company with friends' capital in 1901, and bringing his first product to market in 1903. The razor set was an immediate success, selling nearly 100 000 units in 1904, and an office in London was established in 1905.

> Like many great enterprises, Gillette was founded on the force of one character, King C. Gillette. A salesman for an unrelated business, he had long been looking for a consumer product with which to establish his fortune.

The company changed its name to Gillette in the 1950s, although its founder had long since sold out. By then it was the leading US razor and blade company, its renown based on its superior products and extensive advertising and sponsorship. From then until the 1980s it continued to invest in its core business, fighting off competition through product development, and extending its range to include related lines such as shaving foam and Braun electric razors, and buying into other consumer areas such as Waterman and Paper Mate pens.

GILLETTE IN 1989

It was a story of two halves. The underlying businesses were performing very well, as market share and profits were driven up by product and distribution excellence. In the mirror world of Wall Street, however, the years of steady growth and the conservative balance sheet were condemned as "mature". A number of corporate raiders sized up the business and some were bought off, at the cost of massively leveraging via stock repurchases. Interest cover had dropped from eight times to under four times in two years.

Does the company provide value to its customers?

Gillette's operations in 1988 were split as follows:

%	Sales	Profits
Blades and razors	32	61
Toiletries and cosmetics	28	14
Stationery	11	9
Braun	23	13
Oral-B	6	3

Gillette was the world's top seller of writing instruments (fountain pens, ball-points, stick pens and Liquid Paper), and one of the leading sellers of toiletries and toothbrushes in a number of important international markets. An unrelated business, oil and gas, was being discontinued. While the Braun division marketed a number of branded household appliances, its principal products were electric razors. Toiletries and cosmetics included Right Guard deodorants, hair and skincare products, but also shaving creams and aftershaves. Gillette was, therefore, still substantially dependent on shaving for the bulk of its profits.

It had become the world's leading shaving company in the 1920s and sustained this market dominating position in the decades since, one of the very few consumer-goods companies to do so. Customers valued a smooth shave and were unwilling to switch brands unless there were obvious gains. Gillette forestalled switching by constantly innovating its basic product. The small "investment" required to buy the razor was also a significant barrier to switching.

Does the management provide value to the company?

Colman Mockler and his team had been in charge of the company since 1976. Exiting unrelated businesses, like oil and gas, they had three areas of focus. First, to keep Gillette ahead of its competition by customer-oriented product innovation; second, to improve distribution and market share internationally; and third, to keep working capital, capital expenditure, and overheads tight. As we will see, they succeeded in each aim. Warren Buffett later said of Mockler that he combined integrity, courage, and modesty with exceptional business ability.

Does the company provide value to its shareholders?

$100 invested in Gillette stock in 1978 would have been worth $828 ten years later, a 24 per cent appreciation p.a. or twice the compounded level of comparable stock indices. Earnings had been flat in the 1970s on modest growth in both profits and the number of shares outstanding. Profits growth had been accelerating somewhat for two years and earnings per share even more so as the company began aggressively repurchasing its own stock.

SOURCES OF INFORMATION

Gillette was a business that needed no introduction. It was the owner of the dominant shaving brands, Gillette, Atra, Trac II, and Braun, as well as leading brands in its other markets, and Buffett often commented that the industry and company economics were easy to understand. Men and women needed to shave . . . they preferred to use the best, affordable products . . . citizens of developing countries were rapidly saying the same thing . . . and that was it.

Although Gillette has been compared to Coca-Cola and Wrigley, as a long-lasting dominant consumer franchise it is rather different. All rely on advertising-led branding and superior distribution, but Wrigley and Coke basically manufacture the same products they did 50 years ago. If Gillette had not fundamentally replenished its product line every decade or so, it would no longer exist.

> **Men and women needed to shave . . . they preferred to use the best, affordable products . . . citizens of developing countries were rapidly saying the same thing . . . and that was it.**

The 1988 annual report confirmed management's progress in the three goals mentioned above. Product innovation was at a peak with advances in twin-blade pivoting-head systems and disposable razors. Disposables had been introduced by Bic in the 1970s, and while they were a lower margin product than traditional "razor systems", Gillette had realized the tactical necessity of covering the whole market and soon dominated this segment also.

Like the other Berkshire investments, American Express, Coca-Cola, and McDonald's, Gillette was an American company dominating its home markets and starting to do the same abroad. American sales had grown by a respectable 29 per cent in four years, foreign sales and profits 77 per cent. As important, while gross margin had remained at 58 per cent, operating margin had pulled ahead from 15 per cent to 17 per cent. The combined result of increasing sales, better margins, and share repurchases in those four years was a doubled earnings per share.

> **If Gillette had not fundamentally replenished its product line every decade or so, it would no longer exist.**

QUESTIONS TO TEST YOUR UNDERSTANDING

Do you understand why people buy the product?

"It's pleasant to go to bed every night knowing there are 2.5 billion males in the world who will have to shave in the morning."
Warren Buffet, *Forbes*, 1993

People bought Gillette razors and blades to shave their faces and other body hair. Shaving is not quite as old as mankind but daily shaving by most men has particularly accelerated this century, together with notions of hygiene and personal grooming. Many other Gillette products – deodorants, hair sprays, toothbrushes, even premium pens – fed, and were fed by, the same trends. People would carry on shaving and future product development, whether enhancements to the safety razor or electrical substitutes, seemed to have been anticipated by the company.

How would the industry change in the next ten years?

Shaving is a personal pursuit and consumers would demand the best and safest product at a reasonable price. As already mentioned, it was not good enough to invent a good product and rely on it for decades. The evidence was that management anticipated market needs by innovation or copied competitors' innovations and dominated them. The company had the best global distribution system in the market, but would doubtless extend it to cater for the rapidly developing export markets.

> Shaving is almost as old as mankind but daily shaving by most men has particularly accelerated this century, together with notions of hygiene and personal grooming. Many other Gillette products – deodorants, hair sprays, toothbrushes, even premium pens – fed, and were fed by, the same trends.

Are you comfortable with the management?

Mockler and the other senior managers had shown that they understood the dynamics of their core businesses by concentrating on product innovation, better distribution and marketing, and cost control. They had made small, relevant acquisitions and divested unrelated or unprofitable businesses. A key test of their attitude to shareholders had been the proxy fights of the late 1980s:

Green and white knights

Although Gillette's business fundamentals were stronger than ever, in relative terms its stock languished. Its p/e had fluctuated between ten and 20, often settling around 15. It had not borrowed much and was therefore a good target for the typical late 1980s corporate raider.

> The evidence was that management anticipated market needs by innovation or copied competitors' innovations and dominated them.

Funded by high yield bonds and bank debt, companies like Revlon and funds like KKR sought ungeared companies at low prices. Their theory was that the high free cashflow of a business like Gillette would quickly pay down takeover debt, especially if costs were cut and research deferred. Not all raiders wished to proceed to a full takeover. Sometimes the threat of takeover was enough to persuade incumbent management to follow the bidder's wish. Sometimes the raider took a fee to go away or sold his/her stock back to the company (greenmail) or to a friendlier investor (a white knight).

Gillette's management had been challenged in these ways four times by 1988. On the last two occasions it bought back almost $1.3 billion in stock in order to make raiders go away and to leverage the balance sheet to such an extent that no other debt-funded bidder would be interested. A number of companies had done the same to protect management jobs. Buffett's view in Gillette's case, and several others such as Salomon, USAir and Champion, is that the raiders were trying to buy control on the cheap. Stockholders in general would do better by holding on and waiting for the market to catch up (remember Mr Market). Buffett appreciated management's defence against low bidders and greenmailers. Paradoxically, the high gearing succeeded in scaring off the raiders as well as some conventional investors and the share price fell throughout 1988. No doubt this also attracted Buffett.

Are there substitutes?

There were no substitutes for shaving *per se* and abstinence was in long-term decline. There were direct competitors. Schick (owned by Warner-Lambert), Bic, and Wilkinson Sword (from Swedish Match) all had leads in small product niches or individual countries. There were also many generic producers for supermarket, chemist,

> There were no substitutes for shaving *per se* and abstinence was in long-term decline.

and drugstore own labels, but no other company had close to Gillette's total market share, probably over 60 per cent, its distribution reach, its brand recognition, or its product-development spend.

FINANCIAL ANALYSIS

Colman Mockler had been chairman and CEO for over ten years when Buffett came calling. This is what his record looked like:

$ Millions	Sales	Net income	EPS ($)	Net interest expense	L/T debt	Shareholders' equity
1988	3581	269	2.45	101	1675	(85)
1987	3167	230	2.00	82	840	599
1986	2818	181*	1.42	47	915	461
1985	2400	160	1.29	48	436	898
1984	2289	160	1.29	35	443	791
1983	2183	146	1.19	33	278	757
1982	2239	135	1.11	46	293	721
1981	2334	124	1.03	63	259	720
1980	2315	124	1.03	50	280	717
1979	1985	111	0.92	29	249	648

* Before special charges

Sales had grown 80 per cent or 7 per cent p.a., and net income a more satisfactory 142 per cent or 10 per cent p.a. The share repurchases boosted EPS growth to 166 per cent or 11 per cent p.a. These growth rates had accelerated significantly in the last five years – 12 per cent p.a., 14 per cent p.a., and an enviable 17 per cent p.a. respectively. Growth had been even higher in the last two years.

Consolidated balance sheet, 1988

$ Millions	
Cash and similar	175
Receivables	729
Inventories	653
Fixed assets	683
Other	355
Intangibles	272
Total assets	2868
Debt	1961
Payables	669
Other	323
Total liabilities	2953
Shareholders' equity	(85)

Gillette's balance sheet is straightforward. Supporting $3.6 billion in sales it had predictable levels of working capital – all elements c.$700 million or about two months' worth. The only other large operating item was property, plant, and equipment of around $700 million, low for a manufacturer on this scale. There was a small amount of acquired goodwill (from Braun and some dental endorsements), but not enough to distort the statements.

The big anomalies to take into account in this analysis are the levels of debt and equity. These are explained when we turn to the last three years' cashflows:

Cashflow, 1986–8

These can be condensed as follows:

$ Millions	1988	1987	1986
Net income before exceptionals	269	230	154
Working capital	(206)	(67)	(138)
Capital expenditure	(189)	(147)	(199)
Other	43	111	26
Depreciation and amortization	141	126	108
Dividends	(95)	(85)	(86)
Stock repurchases	(855)	(60)	(568)
Cash generated	(892)	108	(703)

Essentially working capital, capital expenditure, and dividends absorbed all of the net income before exceptionals and depreciation. This is not unusual in such a fast-growing business in the manufacturing sector. Capital expenditure looked high compared to the existing plant investment but, as we will see, this investment was earning high returns, so the more the merrier. Overall operations were cash neutral and this level of growth could easily be sustained. The obvious cash guzzler was stock repurchases. While these were entirely discretionary the business could not have sustained more than two or three more years at this level. In fact, the repurchases had already done the job and made the stock unattractive to debt-funded bidders. Gillette had replaced equity with debt but the underlying operations had so far not been affected.

Consolidated statement of income, 1986–8

$ Millions	1988	1987	1986
Sales	3581	3167	2818
Gross profit	2094	1824	1634
Operating profit	614	523	408
Net interest payable	(101)	(82)	(47)
Other	(64)	(50)	(303)
Income before tax	449	392	58
Net income	269	230	16
EPS ($)	2.45	2.00	0.12
			($1.42 before special charges)

We have already considered the product mix. What about the geo-graphical split?

$ Millions	Europe	Latin America	Other	Total foreign	USA	Total (minus other expenses)
1988						
Sales	1467	378	485	2330	1251	3581
Operating profit	228	102	83	412	230	613
1987						
Sales	1264	318	419	2001	1166	3167
Operating profit	186	77	80	342	206	523
1986						
Sales	1030	307	381	1717	1101	2818
Operating profit	123	67	63	253	183	408

Note: These profits exclude special provisions. The totals include some allowance for central costs.

Although operating margins were slightly higher in the USA than abroad, in both cases they were rising – from 16.6 per cent to 18.4 per cent at home and from 14.7 per cent to 17.7 per cent abroad in two years. The most important trend was sales growth, 27 per cent in two years and mostly abroad. In fact, Gillette had one of the best distribution networks of any American company with manufacturing operations in 28 countries and sales in 200; three-quarters of group employees worked outside the USA.

We have already noted the control of overheads relative to sales growth. The explosion in interest expense is the other interesting element. The $138 million payable in 1988 was misleadingly low because the bulk of stock repurchases happened late in the year. Interest cover was under four times in the fourth quarter.

Owner earnings

Gillette is a good example of how difficult it is to estimate owner earnings. Because of the growth of the business it was absorbing as much in capital formation as it was producing. This is not unusual but provides no guide to the likely free cashflow if the business were to stop growing.

SOURCES OF CAPITAL

Capital expenditure and the growth in working capital were high compared to net income, and net income plus depreciation. That is why the operating business was cash neutral – but this was a function of the growth rate. The *actual* level of plant and working capital was low relative to earnings. Operating assets of $1.4 billion (receivables plus inventories and plant minus payables) generated operating profit, before interest, tax and dividends, of $600 million, a 26 per cent return, assuming a 40 per cent tax rate. This is impressive and implies an economic goodwill attributable to assets not on the balance sheet – brands, market share, the distribution system, and product development.

The fixed-asset base, in particular, was low: $700 million of property, plant and equipment produced $3.6 billion in sales and $600 million

Return on equity

$ Millions	Net income	Operating profit	Shareholders' equity	Long-term debt	Average total capital	ROE – average (%)	Return on capital; average, after tax (%)
1984	159	352	791	443	1135	21	19
1985	160	380	898	436	1284	19	18
1986	173	411	461	915	1355	25	18
1987	230	523	599	840	1408	44	22
1988	269	614	(83)	1675	1515	105	24

Note: The last column is operating profit, minus a notional 40 per cent tax, divided by the average total of shareholders' equity and long-term debt.

operating profit. Impressive ratios for what most people would have thought of as a "capital-intensive" business.

Gillette could not demonstrate free cashflow. More interesting is the rate at which it could reinvest such cash as it retained. If a company is forced to retain cash, whether it is growing or not, it most likely will be earning a low return on its capital and will be destroying shareholder value. If a company can use capital for growth, and earn high rates on it, it is likely to be creating value. In Gillette's case the waters are muddied by the hefty retirement of shareholders' equity – one cannot calculate ROE if the E is negative. In this case we must consider return on capital, too.

The increase in ROE illustrates how it is possible to flatter returns simply by increasing gearing. The ROE of around 20 per cent in 1984/5 is likely to be more accurate since gearing was relatively low in those years. As a guide to more recent years the fully taxed return on average capital, increasing here from 18–19 per cent to 24 per cent, is consistent with the improving performance we saw in the business with further capital being employed at high returns.

How will the *incremental principle* fare? Again, it is hard to employ when shareholders' equity is reducing but another parallel with total capital is possible:

$ Millions	Change in fully taxed operating profit	Change in total capital employed
1984	17	199
1985	14	100
1986	22	42
1987	69	63
1988	55	151
Total	177	555

From the beginning of 1984 to the end of 1988 the business employed $555 million extra capital (long-term debt plus equity). Fully taxed operating profits increased by $177 million. Therefore, the incremental return on incremental capital was 32 per cent.

What was Gillette worth?

Net income in 1988 was $269 million. Berkshire Hathaway made its investment in July 1989. The first quarter's operating results were moderately up, flattered at the per-share level by the dramatic reduction in the number of shares outstanding. It is unlikely that Buffett would have assumed a much higher earnings base than say $2.70, 1988's $2.45 plus 10 per cent. We have calculated a return on average total capital of 24 per cent for 1988 and an IP for incremental capital of 32 per cent. Buffett emphasizes that the precise numbers do not matter, merely that you have a respectable margin of safety. Settling for the conservative 24 per cent, with the knowledge that returns were increasing, achieves this aim.

> Gillette was an efficient user of capital, particularly its long-term assets, and was likely to employ further large amounts of cash at returns above 24 per cent. Goodwill and its amortization were relatively insignificant.

Everything qualitative suggested that the management was in control, market share was dominant, and that foreign earnings would continue to rise. Gillette was an efficient user of capital, particularly its long-term assets, and was likely to employ further large amounts of cash at returns above 24 per cent. Goodwill and its amortization were relatively insignificant. The only negative factor was the high level of indebtedness, which made the enterprise risky.

Assuming there was an answer to this problem, what was intrinsic value? Gillette could employ new capital at the conservatively-estimated rate of 24 per cent. An average company might reinvest and achieve 10 per cent p.a. Gillette's earnings were, therefore, worth 2.4 times as much. A 10 per cent bond or stock deserved a p/e of 10, Gillette 24, giving a share price of $65 and a total value of $6.3 billion for the 97 million shares outstanding at the end of 1988.

WHAT BUFFETT DID

In 1989 Berkshire invested in convertible preferred stocks issued by Gillette, USAir (an airline) and Champion International (a paper and timber company). In each case the preferred was issued as a private placement with a feeling that Berkshire was a white knight, giving management time to restructure in the long-term interest of stock-holders. Berkshire had done the same for Salomon in 1987, rescuing it from the predations of Revlon (Gillette's *bête noire*, too) and was to help out American Express similarly in 1991.

While each issue had different terms, Buffett maintained that most value came from the fixed dividend element, while the option to convert into common was a "kicker". Certainly, Buffett distrusts long-term bonds as a class as there is a periodic risk that inflation will diminish their value. Each major bond issue that Berkshire has bought has had a twist – a tax exemption, a discount to face value or a convertible option – such that the price paid still shows a pair of heels to intrinsic value.

The preferred dividend on Gillette was 8¾ per cent at a time when the long Treasury was yielding 8 per cent. This is such a shallow margin of safety that one is forced to conclude that in this case the most valuable part of the security was the convertible option. Berkshire did indeed convert into common stock at the earliest opportunity so this assumption may be right, albeit with hindsight. If Gillette's businesses had deteriorated and the stock had dived there was a good chance that Berkshire would at least maintain its capital. Consider that the $600 million invested immediately de-geared the company, restoring interest cover to a safer level above six times. This is a false comfort in the sense that an obligation to pay dividends replaced an obligation to pay interest. What counts, though, is that the company was less at risk from its senior creditors; and the presence of Berkshire on the shareholders' register would have scared away predators and, therefore, reduced the need to regear.

To get away from hindsight let us consider the value of the security in its original state and then after conversion in 1991, when Berkshire could have sold its common stock.

In 1989 Berkshire invested $600 million in an 8¾ per cent fixed income security. It was redeemable after ten years and had the right to convert into common at $50 per share. As suggested its fixed income characteristics valued it only slightly above a treasury bond – while it was better than cash, it was only marginally better. It was certainly true that the downside was limited. Unlike the other preferreds in which Berkshire invested in 1989, Buffett and Munger had a good grasp of Gillette's economics, and had little doubt that the dividend would be serviced and redemption met. We have calculated that the intrinsic value per share at that time was $65. A conversion option at $50 only gave a margin of safety of 23 per cent. Buffett's reasoning was no doubt that the very limited downside justified the lower than normal upside. It was a classic Buffett judgment – some chance of gain for no chance of pain.

WHAT HAPPENED NEXT

If this approach was a gamble, Buffett later classed it as a bad one. Excluding dividends, Berkshire's $600 million investment was worth $4.8 billion by the end of 1997, an eightfold appreciation. Some mistake! Buffett meant that he had been too clever. If instead of buying a hybrid security with conversion rights at $50 per share he had negotiated a direct purchase of new common stock he would have paid no more than $40 per share. Compared to our estimated intrinsic value of

> If this approach was a gamble, Buffett later classed it as a bad one. Excluding dividends, Berkshire's $600 million investment was worth $4.8 billion by the end of 1997, an eightfold appreciation. Some mistake!

$65, this would have provided a respectable margin of safety of 38 per cent and he would have ended up with 25 per cent more shares: $600 million converted at $50 per share bought 12 million shares. $600 million invested at $40 per share would have bought 15 million shares. Berkshire would have lost two years of preferred dividend and received a lower common dividend, a net loss of about $70 million. The extra 3 million shares would today be worth $1.2 billion.

What happened in the underlying business to drive up the common stock so far? Gillette sold more blades, razors, cosmetics, and pens in more places at a higher profit. The immediate story was this:

$ Millions	1988	1989	Growth (%)	1990	Growth (%)
Sales	3581	3819	7	4344	14
Operating profit	614	664	8	773	16
EPS ($)	2.45	2.70	10	3.20	19

In 1989, after Berkshire had made its investment, the Sensor razor was announced and was quickly accepted in many national markets as the leading shaving system. Profit gains made from blades and razors were equaled by other segments and surpassed by Braun and Oral-B. The USA was not a mature market, but foreign growth continued to be faster.

The second decision

In April 1991 Gillette gave notice to redeem Berkshire's preferred. The common stock was trading at around $70 so the right to convert into 12 million shares would give a market value of $840 million. Excluding the preferred dividends received so far, the paper profit was $240 million. It was necessary to make another decision, whether to bank the profit by selling the shares or to keep them. The second decision was easier than the initial investment choice. Buffett and Munger knew the business a lot better (Buffett was now on the board), had seen the successful launch of Sensor and the growth in other segments, and were comfortable that they part-owned what they later called an *"inevitable"* – a business whose sales and earnings would inevitably grow over an investment lifetime.

With this background they were unlikely to cash in but it was still useful to confirm that intrinsic value was growing and that there was a margin of safety. No stock repurchases had been made since 1988 and the lack of this outflow, Berkshire's $600 million investment and a net income figure growing faster than capital expenditure combined to reduce long-term debt to just over $1 billion by the end of 1990. The 1990 results still showed shareholders' equity of only $265 million, too small to deduce a legitimate sustainable ROE measure. The 1990 return on average invested capital was a splendid 38 per cent. The IP measurement is hampered because in 1989 total invested capital reduced. But in both 1988 and 1990 IP for invested capital was around 35 per cent:

$ Millions	Taxed operating profits	Change in taxed operating profits	Change in total capital invested	IP for capital (%)
1990	464	66	200	33
1989	398	30	(479)	–
1988	368	54	151	36

We will use the more conservative 35 per cent as the sustainable return to investment. The 1990 EPS was $3.20 to give an intrinsic value of:

$$\$3.20 \times \frac{35\%}{(10\%)^2} = \$112$$

At the then market price of $70, this is a margin of safety of 38 per cent (and a margin of 55 per cent to the conversion price).

Gillette 1991–7

Parker Pen was acquired for $458 million in 1993. A Gillette branded range of shaving toiletries was launched. SensorExcel, from 1993, and SensorExcel for Women, from 1996, further advanced the company's lead in shaving systems. Oral-B dental products, bolstered by small acquisitions and an endless stream of new products, continued to be the fastest growing segment. Blades and razors were still the biggest segment.

The basic values of Gillette were unchanged. Ever-increasing pro-portions of revenues were earned from products launched within five years and from non-US markets, 49 per cent and 63 per cent respec-tively in 1997. The biggest move had been the acquisition of Duracell, the world leader in alkaline batteries, in late 1996. Duracell earned $450 million before tax that year and Gillette acquired it for 110 mil-lion new shares, with a market value of around $11 billion. The benefits to Gillette were clear – another world-class consumer products business with a record of innovation. Combined sales and distribution costs could be cut, with many of the same customers taking products from all parts of the enlarged group. Duracell was not as strong outside the USA, and Gillette could use its on-the-ground operations to promote its new operation globally. Early signs were encouraging with Duracell's sales and contribution increasing by 10 per cent and 17 per cent respectively in 1997.

Overall Gillette had produced the following:

$ Millions	Sales	Net income	EPS ($)	Shareholders' equity	ROE (%)	Year-end share price
1997	10 062	1427	2.49	4841	29	100
1996	9 698	1232	2.16	4471	27	78
1995	8 834	1069	1.89	3879	28	52
1994	7 935	919	1.64	3257	28	37
1993	7 085	772	1.38	2582	30	30
1992	6 752	676	1.24	2538	27	28
1991	6 188	541	1.03	2134	25	28
1990	5 709	388	0.73	607	64	16

Notes: Results are before exceptional charges. The Duracell acquisition was accounted for as a merger. All historical results are restated as if Duracell had always been in the group. Net income is understated because of the amortization of goodwill.

Berkshire's $600 million investment in 1989, excluding dividends, was worth $4.8 billion at the end of 1997, a compounded annual rate of return of 28 per cent.

Gillette has launched a new blade system in 1998.

EXERCISES

1 Assuming that Gillette spent 10 per cent of its sales on research and development how would your calculation of its value in 1988 change if the company decided to capitalize this cost?

2 What if it became more productive and could produce the same results with only half the research budget?

Further questions for discussion

3 Assume: Gillette only sold razor blades; they had to be replaced weekly; the 3 billion men in the world all bought the product; and Gillette's net profit on each blade was ten cents. What is the total profit? Which of these assumptions is least likely?

4 Suppose Gillette decided to keep its brands and contract out all other activity, only earning licence fees. What risks would it be incurring? How could its suppliers improve their negotiating positions?

The Walt Disney Company

Berkshire Hathaway owned stock in Capital Cities from 1977 to 1980 and in ABC from 1978 to 1979, and again from 1984. In 1986, Berkshire bought a large stake in Capital Cities to enable it to purchase ABC. Capital Cities/ABC merged with Disney in 1996, with Berkshire receiving some stock and some cash. It bought more Disney stock in the market that year.

HISTORY

American Broadcasting Companies (ABC)

This was a spin-off from the motor force of American radio and television technology, RCA. The latter owned NBC as well and was ordered by the FCC to divest one of its networks. Edward Noble bought ABC in 1943. It was the weakest of the three networks with little original programming and few affiliated local stations for the following two decades. Merging with United Paramount Theaters in 1953, it started to commission programs from Hollywood, gain affiliates, and improve its scheduling. It was briefly the most watched network in the 1970s and has remained in the top three since. It bought the leading sports cable channel, ESPN, in 1984.

Capital Cities

This started as a one-TV and one-radio-station company in Albany, New York in 1954. The TV station's first manager, Tom Murphy, became the driving force of the company and with his partner, Dan Burke, went on the acquisition trail. Thirty corporate purchases later they managed a TV, radio, magazine, and newspaper empire. By the time they bought ABC in 1986, Murphy and Burke had a reputation as the best management team in the media industry, and the tightest.

Walt Disney

The Disney story deserves some space. He was an animator who had an unhappy, violent childhood and spent the rest of his life trying to create perfect environments for children. He started a Hollywood studio with his brother Roy in 1923. Walt was the creative one while Roy handled the numbers, but they both learned a hard lesson early. They had assigned the copyright of their first successful character, Oswald the Lucky Rabbit, to their distributor, but were soon cut out of the production process as the distributor commissioned cheaper artists to continue the series. This was good grounding in intellectual-property realities. The next character Walt created he was careful to retain and exploit in the name of the studio only. This was Mickey Mouse, a twentieth-century phenomenon.

No studio can fail that pays its biggest star in cheese.

No studio can fail that pays its biggest star in cheese. Mickey was a worldwide success. Distributed globally by Columbia, but with the copyright retained by Disney, the studio had to produce one cartoon per month to keep up with demand. Walt pioneered merchandising in Hollywood. He published *The Mickey Mouse Book* and licensed the character to a syndicated cartoon strip, breakfast cereals and the famous watches. The Disneys realized that there was no end to what they had started. Mickey was joined by Donald Duck, a more cynical and eventually more successful character than Mickey, Goofy, and the others.

The Disney brothers' next big venture was the first full-length animated feature, *Snow White and the Seven Dwarfs*. It ran way over budget and Roy had to bully and plead until the Bank of America stumped up almost $1 million to finish it. The film was a giant success, grossing $8.5 million on its first run. The Disneys' company went public in 1940, but continued to take enormous financial risks until Walt's death in 1966. He had indebted the studio to make further animated films in the 1940s, many of which flopped. World War Two flattened the business, since already almost half its income came from abroad. The live-action nature films from 1948 and the hugely successful children's shows on television (mainly ABC) from the mid-1950s revived the company in time for Walt's last big risk.

He wanted to create a place for families, a haven of safety and fun. Disneyland in California was refused funding by the studio that bore his name so he started it as a private and secret project. It cost $17 million, one-third of which was guaranteed by ABC, but even before it opened in 1955 its strengths were apparent. Corporate sponsors lined up to be associated with the most popular children's characters in the country and a large part of the capital budget and running costs were covered in advance. The studio quietly absorbed this forbidden triumph and Walt moved on to imagine Disney World.

After Walt's death the business drifted. Disney World was opened successfully in 1971, the same year Roy died, and some non-animated films were released, but the film business soon dried up and the company survived on theme-park income. Roy's son, Roy E. Disney, encouraged the property developer Sid Bass to take a large minority stake in 1984 and together they installed Michael Eisner and Frank Wells as the new management team. Eisner and Wells knew that there was treasure buried under the Magic Castle. By 1986 they were exploiting the library on video and through cinema rereleases, dramatically improving the theme-park returns by advertising, increasing prices, and building hotels, and reviving non-animated cinema and TV programming. They also had plans to reestablish Disney as the premier animation studio.

> After Walt's death the business drifted. Disney World was opened successfully in 1971, the same year Roy died, and some non-animated films were released, but the film business soon dried up and the company survived on theme-park income.

CAPITAL CITIES IN 1986

Tom Murphy and Dan Burke had realized in the 1960s that TV stations and some other media businesses were what Buffett called *franchises*. They required little capital expenditure, were relatively impervious to competition, were subject to growing demand from the public and advertisers and had strong pricing power. There is more on the nature of local TV stations in Chapter 17 on the *Washington Post*. Cap Cities had a wide spread of stations, ranking high in the ratings and run at low cost. It had been selectively buying broadcasting and publishing assets for decades, but only at times when prices were reasonable. The management was also hot on expense control and often took the knife aggressively to acquired companies, aware that they could supply management if incumbent staff disagreed. By 1985 they had a company earning $150 million, five times the level ten years earlier, with the same proportion of debt to equity, but with 15 per cent fewer shares outstanding. Cap Cities had earned around 20 per cent on its equity since the mid-1970s. The capital gain on its shares, excluding dividends, was eight times or a remarkable 26 per cent p.a.

Cap Cities paid $3.4 billion cash, and a small amount in warrants, for ABC in early 1986. To finance this it used $750 million of its own cash, borrowed $1.35 billion and sold certain media and real estate properties for $788 million. The gap was filled by Berkshire, which bought 3 million new shares, or 19 per cent of the enlarged total, for $518 million. At the time this was one of the largest ever mergers in the USA. Cap Cities had paid an apparent 20 times 1985 earnings for ABC and many thought that this was a deal too far.

In fact, this was an excellent deal for Cap Cities and Berkshire. Strategically, Cap Cities had captured a major supplier further up the distribution chain. Financially, it was better than it appeared, even before post-merger cost cutting. A pro forma 1985 combination of Cap Cities and ABC would have showed the following:

THE WALT DISNEY COMPANY

$ Millions	
Revenues	4089
Operating costs	(3371)
Depreciation	(93)
Amortization of intangibles	(55)
Operating income	570
Net interest	(186)
Income before taxes	384
Net income	175
Net income before amortization	230

This is not a precise reckoning as it includes certain post-merger adjustments of program rights. Berkshire had paid a price that valued the combination at $2.8 billion or, prima facie, a p/e of only 12: very respectable for a growing business with a historic ROE of c.20 per cent.

The post-merger experience of Cap Cities/ABC was excellent:

$ Millions	1985	1994	Annualized growth rate (%)
Revenues	4089	6379	5.1
Operating costs	(3371)	(4968)	4.4
Depreciation	(93)	(109)	1.8
Amortization	(55)	(63)	1.5
Operating income	570	1239	9.0
Net interest	(186)	(34)	(20.8)
Income before taxes	384	1205	13.5
Net income	175	680	16.3
EPS ($)	1.09	4.42	16.8

Cap Cities had grown its revenues gradually. Its secret was lower down the income statement. A respectable 9 per cent p.a. growth in operating income is transformed by the lower interest charge into an excellent per-share result. The business had clearly been generating cash and paying down its debt. Also interesting is the modest growth in depreciation costs which implies low capital formation.

DISNEY IN 1995

Over at Disney, Michael Eisner and Frank Wells had been applying their own skills. Disney's own recent record looked like this:

$ Millions	1989	1995	Annualized growth rate (%)
Revenues	4594	12 112	17.5
Operating income	1229	2 446	12.2
Net income	703	1 380	11.9
EPS ($)	1.27	2.60	12.7

This progression is not as attractive as that for Cap Cities mainly because of the effect of Eurodisney. Disney had very effectively operated theme parks in the USA and Japan for decades. Eurodisney, which opened in 1992, is the European equivalent of Disneyland. It was an organic outgrowth of the existing strategy. It was financed through an off-balance sheet structure. Disney held 49 per cent and institutional and private shareholders the balance; a large amount of debt, non-recourse to Disney, was also raised. Disney would earn a return as shareholder plus significant royalty and management fee income. This was halfway between the American practice of wholly-owned and operated parks and the Japanese model, which paid royalty income only.

> Eurodisney, which opened in 1992, is the European equivalent of Disneyland. It was an organic outgrowth of the existing strategy. It was financed through an off-balance sheet structure.

Eurodisney had not met its projections, particularly in hotel occupancy, a key profit driver. The debt was rescheduled in 1994 in a deal that seemed to a number of observers favorable to Disney – the banks blinked first, understandably, since there was no hope of recovery without Disney's support. Nevertheless, the investment told on results, costing $515 million and $110 million in 1993 and 1994 respectively (these were income statement effects, the cash cost was higher). Eurodisney was moving in the right direction. It was a sensible product extension, financed in a way that lowered the risk to Disney. It competed well in Europe and visitor numbers were already high and rising.

Besides, there was a lot more to Disney than this one investment.

Does the company provide value to its customers?

American Express adds to its customers' self-esteem. The Coke bottle embodies many millions of people's aspirations. Disney goes beyond that. It also deals in dreams but, unlike most other businesses, it creates those dreams. Seventy years ago Walt Disney invented a talking mouse and people rushed to watch, watch again, and buy the merchandise that made the relationship permanent. Today children play their "Aladdin" and "Lion King" tapes endlessly. Disney is not the only entertainment company in the world. In a global business dominated by the USA, where the English language and American values are now almost universally aspired to, the same, large Hollywood studios have preserved their hegemony for decades. Even so, Disney has three advantages over its long-lived rivals:

> American Express adds to its customers' self-esteem. The Coke bottle embodies many millions of people's aspirations. Disney goes beyond that. It also deals in dreams but, unlike most other businesses, it creates those dreams.

1 *Children* – its products appeal to an audience that demands satisfaction first time. Parents trust Disney's standards and values. If you wanted a measure of the value of the Disney brand, try this thought experiment. You are a parent taking your young family to a multi-screen cinema and you have the choice of a Disney film at full price or any other film at half price. Which do you choose? The principal risk in film production, where the creative and marketing budget of each project might exceed $100 million, is that it is difficult to predict what will sell. Disney has minimized this risk. And since children are the main audience the studio can rerelease its product to each new generation at little cost;

2 *Licensing* – Disney led the way in licensing its character rights for merchandise. This is a fascinating business. In what other field does a customer pay for the right to advertise the supplier's product? So Disney receives a fee for every pencil case and hamburger carrying Snow White's image, and every such image further promotes the character, the film, and the brand. Disney has the largest character-licensing business in the world;

3 *Talent* – Disney uses fine animators, writers, composers, and actors. Each is replaceable. As we have seen, film production is risky. A common method to reduce this risk is to use famous actors. This gives strength to the actors, or their agents, against the film producers. More of whatever income is generated passes to the talent. When you choose to watch a Disney creation, you care much less about the individual actors or other contributors – the quality must be high but the precise individuals are unimportant. And cheese is cheaper than a share of the gross.

Disney was a weaker proposition in one respect than Coke, Gillette, or the *Washington Post*. Its markets were more crowded. The *Washington Post* is the only important daily paper in its market. Coke and Gillette products are nearly universally available with a cost, quality, and recognition factor that no existing competitor or new entrant can replicate. Disney's brand is mighty and it has a heritage that no other entertainment company can touch (Warner has strong characters but lacks the same consistent identity). But it was not inconceivable that another studio could produce quality children's films, animated or not.

> If you wanted a measure of the value of the Disney brand, try this thought experiment. You are a parent taking your young family to a multiscreen cinema and you have the choice of a Disney film at full price or any other film at half price. Which do you choose?

Does the management provide value to the company?
Does the company provide value to its shareholders?

Eisner and Co. had certainly refocused the business. They had created a string of animated cinema hits, unrivaled since the 1960s. Video rereleases had been cleverly hyped with limited sales windows both provoking demand and ensuring the success of future rereleases to fresh generations. Merchandising had been taken to yet another level with the successful roll-out of The Disney Store format in the USA and internationally. Apart from the not proven verdict in Europe, the theme parks and other resorts had performed as hoped: every film admission or toy sale created another potential visitor. Eisner had built up admissions and prices (for admissions, hotel rooms, and merchandise), realizing that the company had considerable pricing power against an eager clientele. The Disney Channel on cable was a clever way of re-entering TV markets.

There were question marks over Eisner. Wells had died in an accident in early 1994, leaving him effectively in sole command. The company had invested heavily in live-action films and in record production. This was financially successful but unrelated to the Disney brand and core businesses. The new management had done well for stockholders, producing a total return to shareholders of 28 per cent p.a. over ten years. Shareholders had been generous right back. Eisner owned or had options over 1.5 per cent of the company. The options were valued at $170 million, making him one of the best paid employees in the world.

Berkshire Hathaway invests in a number of publicly traded companies that have option schemes. Indeed, practically all quoted companies have them, although Disney's was particularly generous. Berkshire itself has never issued any stock options. Buffett and Munger prefer to tie compensation to factors under managers' control, typically simple volume or key ratio targets. Share prices do not tell you anything about the underlying value or prospects of a business, they simply give you an opportunity to buy or sell according to your own view of intrinsic value. Issuing options is like giving away lottery tickets where the prizes are donated by stockholders.

SOURCES OF INFORMATION

The personal connection

The Buffett Partnership paid $4 million for around 5 per cent of Disney in 1966. This was one of Warren Buffett's first attempts to estimate asset values not carried on the balance sheet. Research took him beyond the financial statements with a visit to Disneyland and a meeting with Walt Disney himself. Buffett and Munger put a value on the film library which was in excess of the market capitalization of the whole company. The partnership took a quick profit, selling out for a 50 per cent gain after one year.

At about the time that Berkshire had to decide to take Disney stock or cash for its stake in Cap Cities, Disney was publishing its results for the year to September 1995. The company was a far bigger beast than it had been in the 1960s, but its constituents would have been familiar to Walt:

$ Millions	Division		
	Filmed entertainment	Theme parks	Consumer products
Revenues	6002	3960	2151
Operating income	1074	861	511

While Filmed Entertainment made not just animated pieces but live action films and TV programs, it was still the heart of the company. It created content – characters, plots, brands – that could be exploited at the theme parks and through merchandising. There were now six theme parks and a number of hotels. Under development were cruise ships and Celebration, a new town.

Entertainment was an increasingly crowded and competitive field but Disney stood above its peers. Its animated films and family programming were the preferred viewing for a significant part of the English-speaking world, while its resorts and theme parks had become number-one destination venues for tourists.

QUESTIONS TO TEST YOUR UNDERSTANDING

Do you understand why people buy the product?

Watch a child in front of a Disney video. Watch it yourself.

How would the industry change in the next ten years?

Disney's values were timeless and universal. Technology was evolving but from Animatronics onwards Disney had stayed ahead of the trend. Distribution challenges would come from satellite, cable, computers, and other new media. Prime content would always find a public.

Are you comfortable with the management?

Disney had been galvanized by Eisner, Wells and a new generation of managers. The step improvements from video releases, Disney stores and a wider production slate had been complemented by more aggressive pricing and cannier marketing. Eisner himself was a brilliant combination of leader, controller, and creator. There was the question of whether he was worth what he was paid. He was the dominant executive at the company. His influence may have been reinforced by the presence of several "independent" directors with personal or commercial links with Eisner or the company.

FINANCIAL ANALYSIS

Disney was offering to buy Capital Cities/ABC, a company half its own size. To understand Buffett's decision at this point we must consider Disney on its own and the enlarged group.

Consolidated balance sheets, 1994 and 1995

$ Millions	1995	1994
Cash and investments	1 943	1 510
Receivables	1 793	1 671
Inventories	824	668
Film and TV[1]	2 099	1 596
Properties	6 723	6 445
Other	1 224	937
Total assets	14 606	12 826
Creditors	2 843	2 475
Debt	2 984	2 937
Tax[2]	1 267	1 206
Unearned income[3]	861	700
Total liabilities	7 955	7 318
Equity	6 651	5 508

Notes to table overleaf

Notes

1. Gone were the days when the film library was not carried on the balance sheet, but it is intriguing given their respective value to the company how the cost of film and TV projects compared to property costs. The latter was far larger, but it is debatable which was more valuable. The ability of the company to capitalize film costs invokes tough accounting questions. Essentially, the product was carried at cost until opening; thereafter, an element was expensed proportionate to the ratio of actual gross to anticipated gross for the period. The major risk was that management overforecast total gross leaving the rump of expense to be taken as a loss. It was comforting that the amount so capitalized did look low. The notes to the accounts also revealed that 87 per cent of unamortized production costs were likely to be expensed within three years. Much of the library was bound to have a shelf life far beyond this.

2. There was a significant deferred tax liability arising from theme-park investment. This was likely to be sustainable or grow as the theme park/resort/other property program continued to develop.

3. Disney received handy amounts of cash from Tokyo Disneyland and other royalty counterparties which were only recognized as income over the life of the agreements.

Sources of capital

From a shareholders' equity base of $6.7 billion, the company generated revenues of $12.1 billion and net income of $1.4 billion. Clearly the factors just referred to – the comparatively low investment in programming, the deferred tax base, and unearned income – were significant free forms of capital. Most important, though, was just being Disney. Being Disney meant that people preferred and paid a premium for your films, videos, cable channel, merchandise, and theme parks.

Return on equity

This was the recent record:

$ Millions	Net income	Average shareholders' equity	ROE (%)	IP (%)
1992	817	4288	19.1	
1993	888	4868	18.2	12.2
1994	1110	5269	21.1	55.4
1995	1380	6080	22.7	33.3

The merger

There were 153.9 million Cap Cities shares outstanding. Disney offered one of its own shares plus $65 in cash for each Cap Cities share. Subject to limitations Cap Cities' shareholders could alternatively elect for all Disney stock or all cash. Disney's stock traded at c.$58 at the time valuing the whole transaction at $19 billion. Cap Cities' nine months' results to October 1, 1995 showed a net income, adjusted for exceptional costs and intangibles, of $573 million. Using a rough pro rata, this equates to $764 million in a full year. A $19 billion price tag gives a p/e of 24.9. Cap Cities' historic IP was c.20 per cent although its current ROE had fallen to 17 per cent. On either measure an exit p/e of 24.9 was more than fair value. Therefore, if Buffett had chosen to elect for cash only he could have rationalized the price.

He did not. He elected for Disney shares only and, postmerger, bought more Disney stock in the market. Why? The most important reason was strategic. Buffett, Eisner and Murphy understood that Disney was the premier content producer in the USA. Cap Cities, with its network and cable interests in particular, was a leading distributor. The combination could create serious value. Buffett played the rare role (for him) of marriage broker, encouraging both managers to think in these terms.

Financially the deal also had to make sense. The combined animal would look quite different in terms of its capital structure depending on whether other Cap Cities' shareholders elected for shares or cash. There would be certain cost savings and unquantifiable benefits. A simple pro forma addition of the two companies' operating incomes, before interest, gave a total of $3,543 million for 1995. Disney had net debt of $1.04 billion pre-merger and Cap Cities had net cash of $700 million. We can consider two scenarios. Both ignore amortization of intangibles and conservatively assume an interest rate of 10 per cent. The tax rate is 35 per cent.

1. What if all Cap Cities' shareholders took cash?

There would be $19.3 billion of debt and no increase in the number of Disney shares from the 524.8 million outstanding. The income statement would look like this:

	$ Millions
Operating income	3543
Interest payable	(1930)
Income before tax	1613
Net income	1048
EPS ($)	2.0

2. What if all Cap Cities' shareholders took one Disney share and $65?

There were 153.9 million Cap Cities shares outstanding so the number of Disney shares would go up to 678.7 million and there would be $10.3 billion debt:

	$ Millions
Operating income	3543
Interest payable	(1030)
Income before tax	2513
Net income	1633
EPS ($)	2.41

Berkshire owned 20 million shares in Cap Cities. It knew it was electing for shares, that there were tax advantages for others to do so and that the deal made sense. Scenario 2 was, therefore, a more likely outcome. Berkshire would receive 20 million Disney shares, 2.95 per cent of the enlarged total, and $1.3 billion in cash.

Buffett says that the most important financial consideration in a share-for-share purchase is that the selling shareholder receives as much value as he or she gives. Berkshire was giving up 13 per cent of Cap Cities (it had sold some of its original 19 per cent) for 2.95 per cent of Disney plus the cash. We have seen that Cap Cities was earning $764 million p.a. with an IP/ROE range of 17–20 per cent. The most generous estimate of intrinsic value (IV) would be $15.3 billion. Berkshire's 13 per cent would be worth $2 billion. Disney's most recent ROE/IP was 23–33 per cent. Assuming that only the low end of this range could be applied to the combination and using scenario 2's net income produces an IV of $37.6 billion. Berkshire's 2.95 per cent would, therefore, be worth $1.1 billion. Together with the $1.3 billion in cash this gave a total value for the transaction to Berkshire of $2.4 billion. This was above the existing $2 billion and took no account of post-merger benefits.

> Buffett says that the most important financial consideration in a share-for-share purchase is that the selling shareholder receives as much value as he or she gives.

Berkshire bought a further 4.6 million Disney shares in the market in early 1996. The purchase price is obscure but is likely to have been between $50 and $60, valuing the enlarged group at $34–41 billion, close to IV. There is no question that Buffett promoted the merger because he saw profound synergistic benefits to both parties. In this instance the margin of safety came from such anticipated but unquantified sources.

WHAT HAPPENED NEXT

Cap Cities' owners did in fact elect for Disney stock and after some minor issuances and repurchases the number of Disney shares outstanding is 671 million. Adding back exceptional items and amortization of goodwill, the Disney story unfolded as follows:

$ Millions	1997	1996	1995
Revenues	22 473	18 739	12 151
Operating income	4 384	3 325	2 227
Interest payable	(693)	(438)	(110)
Income before tax	3 691	2 887	2 117
Net income	2 399	1 877	1 376
EPS ($)	3.49	3.03	2.60

N.B. 1997 was the first full merger year. This explains the lower than anticipated combined operating profit in 1996. From a full-year base of $3.5 billion (derived above), the increase to $4.4 billion in 1997 was superb. Pro forma operating income increased 15–25 per cent in all divisions. The major unanticipated (by us) variance was in interest costs. The 6–7 per cent was far lower than our assumed 10 per cent and this alone added 30 cents to earnings.

Together with some of his other major positions, Buffett trimmed his Disney stake in 1997, selling just over 3 million shares. The remaining 21.6 million were worth $2.1 billion or $99 per share. Excluding dividends this was a growth c.28 per cent p.a. in market value. Berkshire had paid a split-adjusted $17 for its Cap Cities shares in early 1986. They were now worth $99 *and* it had received cash of $65. Again excluding dividends the compound capital gain was some 21 per cent p.a.

EXERCISES

1 Only measuring until 1995, should Buffett have kept the shares he bought in 1966? Assume no shares were issued and ignore dividends.

2 On the same basis what amount would the Disneys need to have invested in 1923 to create the same annualized return by 1995?

Further questions for discussion

3 What characteristics do Disney and Coca-Cola share? How do they differ?

4 Do you think Disney should stick to family entertainment? What are the risks of doing so?

17

The Washington Post Company

Berkshire Hathaway bought 467 250 "B" ordinary stock in The Washington Post Company (WPC) in 1973 for $10.6 million.

HISTORY

The *Washington Post* newspaper was first published in Washington, DC in 1877. Known for its straight editorial policy it flourished from the beginning. It had several owners, most of them politicians, in the following 50 years and soon its reputation had been tarnished by partisanship and a final, doomed attempt to take it downmarket. It went bust in 1933 and Eugene Meyer, a banker, bought it for $825 000. He rebuilt its reputation painstakingly on the back of investment in the best journalists and editors. Washington was a very competitive newspaper market then but the *Post* gradually gained readership, advertising and profitability. Meyer himself turned to politics and was ultimately named head of the Fed. He passed control to his daughter Kay and her talented husband, Philip Graham, in 1948.

> Graham established the *Post* as the leading Washington paper and competitors began to die off. He also bought a radio station, several local TV stations, and the weekly news magazine *Newsweek*.

Graham established the *Post* as the leading Washington paper and competitors began to die off. He also bought a radio station, several local TV stations, and the weekly news magazine *Newsweek*. Suffering from manic depression, regrettably Graham killed himself in 1963, and Kay assumed the role of publisher and president of the board. Moving Ben Bradlee from *Newsweek* to the editor's chair at the *Post*, Graham and her editorial team promoted hard, investigative journalism that cemented the *Post* as the leading Washington paper and gave it a national and international reputation. The company went public in 1971.

WPC IN 1973

The company had three principal sources of earnings in 1973. Half of its operating income was still derived from the newspaper and roughly one-quarter each from *Newsweek* and its broadcast division, one radio and three TV stations. Although the company had bought some of these properties, they had all been well-established businesses in their own right and it was easy enough to answer the three value questions.

Does the company provide value to its customers?

A daily city newspaper has an intimate engagement with its readers. It is their source of news about the world and their neighbors, a window on history and the local bulletin board. Known internationally for the quality of its political journalism the *Post* took care to report thoroughly parochial stories of interest only to Washingtonians. Although there was one smaller daily paper and broadcast media also carried news, to most of its readers the *Post* was indispensable.

> Known internationally for the quality of its political journalism the *Post* took care to report thoroughly parochial stories of interest only to Washingtonians. Although there was one smaller daily paper and broadcast media also carried news, to most of its readers the *Post* was indispensable.

The TV stations were also in a good position. Under FCC rules they enjoyed practical monopolies for their affiliated networks in their areas (CBS in Washington, DC and Jacksonville, Florida, and ABC in Miami, Florida). If you wanted to watch TV in these major areas you were very likely to be watching a WPC station. *Newsweek* was in a more competitive environment, battling against *Time* and *US News & World Report,* as well as many other weekly magazines. It was well established as a leading news magazine with over 50 geographic and demographic editions and a strong subscription base. It had to remain ahead of its competition but clearly provided an attractive product to readers worldwide.

All company properties were well-branded with a distinctive market position and a loyal core of customers.

Does the management provide value to the company?

Kay Graham describes movingly in her memoir how she grew into the role of publisher and businesswoman after her husband's death. Patronized initially both as a woman and the figurehead of a passive family investment, she gradually learned the ropes. Surrounded by first-rate journalists, editorial standards were not a problem, and the broad direction of the company was proving profitable. The *Post* had come to dominate the Washington paper market, the TV stations were seemingly unassailable and *Newsweek* had a strong, profitable market position. Graham and her team demonstrated the quality that had been lacking in the 1930s, integrity. Facing fierce political pressure she OK'd first the publication of the Pentagon Papers, just as WPC went public, and later the Watergate investigation. The political threat was not toothless. President Nixon instructed the FCC to threaten revocation of the broadcast licenses. Graham stood firm; it was the President who fell. Customer trust grew as editorial independence was proved.

> The political threat was not toothless. President Nixon instructed the FCC to threaten revocation of the broadcast licenses. Graham stood firm; it was the President who fell. Customer trust grew as editorial independence was proved.

In some other ways the first decade of Graham's leadership was problematical. At the *Post* (and many other papers) it was questionable whether management or unions were in charge. Spanish customs, overmanning and spiraling pay meant that the newspaper did not meet its profit potential. The *Post* made a $10.5 million operating profit on $112 million, whereas a tighter-run competitor might have made 50 per cent more – the *Post* itself had ten years before. There was also the question of taking the company public. WPC had debt and Graham's family had substantial death duties to pay which meant partial flotation was a sensible option. Graham opted for a two class share structure. She exercised control over a majority of Class "A", which carried most votes. Class "B" had limited voting rights but equivalent economic value. This structure was more common then and allowed family businesses to issue stock without losing control. The system was often abused, however, and "A" holders might retain unusual perks and be dilatory in management without fear of shareholder action. There was no evidence of the former at WPC but cost management *was* slack.

Does the company provide value to its shareholders?

WPC owned first-rate media properties. Although margins were not what they could have been the strategic value of the businesses was such that even average management could have delivered good returns. Class "B" stock had been issued in June 1971 and had almost doubled in the 18 months since. WPC was doing well, producing an ROE of c.19 per cent, and was fairly certain to deliver a rising income.

In 1973 the stock price halved. Nothing had changed in the economics of WPC's three divisions – but the American stock market was collapsing.

SOURCES OF INFORMATION

The personal connection

- *Warren Buffett moved to Washington when he was 13 to join his congressman father. He delivered the* Washington Post *and a competing paper, and also sold magazine subscriptions as he went. Over four years he built up five simultaneous paper routes and earned over $5000. This provided his original investment funds.*
- *Newsprint was in his blood. Warren's father started his career as editor of the* Daily Nebrasken *and his mother's father owned a small weekly paper.*

As the box suggests, Warren Buffett knew all about the *Washington Post*. As with American Express, GEICO, and Coke he was returning to familiar territory. But WPC aside, he had long been fascinated by the possibilities of the newspaper business. In 1973 he was still enamored with classic Ben Graham prescriptions that related intrinsic value to book value. In 1972 Charlie Munger had persuaded him that they should jointly buy See's Candy, a chocolate manufacturer and retailer. Paying over three times book value, he had begun to see the possibilities of economic goodwill. A business requiring little capital with good growth prospects might be very valuable at the right price. See's prospects were tied to the quality of its product and service. Buffett saw that some types of business had an even stronger lock on their customers. An unregulated monopoly would be ideal: these were scarce. Next best, a franchise, a business that could price aggressively against its customers and suppliers but still repel competition.

The newspaper business fitted the bill. Unlike Britain, with its dominant national dailies, America had a regional newspaper structure. Every town had its own newspaper or newspapers. Buffett learned his lesson first-hand. One of Berkshire's first acquisitions had been the Omaha *Sun*, a local paper. Although it was a good product it was unable to raise its cover price without hurting circulation. Buffett calculated the following:

Date	Cities with daily papers	Cities with >1 paper
1910	1207	689
1971	1511	37

The *Sun* was Omaha's second paper and that fatally weakened its economics; it was sold. What Buffett wanted was a market-dominant paper. His research had shown that such a paper would soon drive out competition. This would give it pricing power. Readers would be dependent and not sensitive to rises in cover prices. Advertisers would also be captured. Television was substantially a national medium and radio was too diffuse. If you advertised in the local paper you were certain to reach a high per centage of households. No other medium could promise the same.

Buffett later developed key drivers to measure a paper's effectiveness, the *penetration ratio* – the per centage of households in the area regularly buying the paper – and the *news hole* – the per centage of total space dedicated to news. A high news hole makes a paper more attractive to its readers, increasing penetration, and a high penetration ratio makes a paper more attractive to advertisers.

At this distance we have little information on the *Post*'s key drivers, but we can be sure that Warren Buffett knew them by heart. The annual report did contain some useful information, though. There was no daily competitor but an evening paper with a Sunday edition, the *Washington Star*, had a circulation at c.65 per cent of the *Post*'s level. It was in the same position as the *Sun* had been, unlikely to be getting the cream of advertising or cover price dollars. The *Post*'s own circulation was rising gently, particularly on Sunday which was an attractive day for advertisers. The cover price was rising above the inflation rate. The number of advertising lines was also growing and the revenue per line was growing fast.

> A high news hole makes a paper more attractive to its readers, increasing penetration, and a high penetration ratio makes a paper more attractive to advertisers.

The company published little information on its television stations but they also took in large amounts of advertising revenue, c.70 per cent of it national. Television was fast becoming the most important way for national advertisers to reach the whole of the USA as more people owned televisions each year and they spent more time watching them; the number of households owning a set had doubled over the previous decade. There were three dominant broadcast networks and each of them was reliant on its affiliated local stations. These were near-monopoly broadcasters in their local towns and cities. The growth in viewing and the resulting surge in advertising in a medium with some monopoly characteristics gave the franchise quality Buffett desired.

Newsweek was in a competitive market, particularly with *Time*, but Buffett would also have liked what he saw. The weekly news

magazines were "well read", that is readers paid attention to the content. National and, increasingly, international in circulation they
had the flexibility to tailor editorial and advertising content to different geographic and demographic markets. This was because 90 per
cent of sales were by subscription and, therefore, to identified categories of readers, valuable to advertisers.
Newsweek had been growing its circulation and
advertising pages gradually each year. Like its
sister paper advertising and circulation revenue
had been growing fast, c.10 per cent p.a.

> **It probably sounds by now that all media properties were golden eggs. But this was only true of market-dominant media.**

Newsweek had also been slowly growing its market share. It had one
other attraction not shared with the other WPC businesses – its
"float". Selling 90 per cent of your circulation in advance gave the
advantage of certainty to production management. It also generated
a large amount of cash from subscriptions received in advance. None
of WPC's businesses required that much capital but *Newsweek* was
actually a net capital contributor.

It probably sounds by now that all media properties were golden
eggs. But this was only true of market-dominant media. Second-string
papers were weak. So, probably, were radio stations. WPC owned one
about which information is scant. It appears to have accounted for
under 1 per cent of total revenues. Radio was competitive since the
number of broadcasters was not culled by economics (like papers) or
regulation (like TV).

Questions to test your understanding

Do you understand why people buy the product?

The paper sold because it was the premier way for people in
Washington to learn about their city and the world. Advertisers bought
space because there were few other ways of ensuring so many local
people would get the message. The TV stations sold advertising time
because companies had few alternatives if they wanted to speak to the
whole of America. The news magazine sold advertising because it was

successful in identifying groups of readers that advertisers wanted to target; readers got a convenient and authoritative digest of world news.

How would the industry change in the next ten years?

If quality was maintained the *Post* would increase its dominance in Washington and gain a higher share of circulation and advertising revenue. The Nixon threat to the TV licenses was already receding in 1973, and if their licenses continued to be renewed – usually a formality – they would continue to have a lock on a growing share of national advertising spend with little capital requirement. Cable systems were just starting but were very expensive to roll out and were enjoying low penetration rates; a possible threat to monitor. *Newsweek* prospered in a competitive market. Weekly magazines would continue to be a competitive market in which well-managed titles should grow.

Are you comfortable with the management?

Kay Graham acted with integrity and she clearly had some talented managers around her. She had made some questionable operational and capital decisions but the media properties she controlled were very well positioned and were being expanded.

Are there substitutes?

People could dispense with the paper or switch off the TV but were unlikely to. Advertisers could find other routes to consumers (cable, direct mail, skywriting) but a dominant newspaper or a network-affiliated station were likely to be first choices. *Newsweek* had many substitutes but a loyal and growing readership would probably allow it to hold its own – they could find substitutes but seemed to prefer what they had.

FINANCIAL ANALYSIS

After the sale of Class "B" shares, WPC declared the following results:

$ Millions	1973	1972
Advertising	188.5	166.1
Circulation	54.6	47.4
Other	3.9	4.3
Total revenues	246.9	217.8
Operating costs	(164.7)	(146.6)
Selling and admin.	(53.0)	(46.3)
Deprec. and amort.	(3.6)	(3.1)
Total costs	(221.3)	(196.0)
Operating income	25.7	21.8
Net interest	0.1	(1.7)
Affiliates	1.0	0.5
Other	(0.2)	(0.4)
Income before taxes	26.6	20.2
Current tax	(10.6)	(7.5)
Deferred tax	(2.7)	(2.7)
Total tax provision	(13.2)	(10.2)
Net income	13.3	10.0

Note: 1972 excludes a small extraordinary item

Balance sheet figures are harder to get hold of after 25 years, but a rough reconstruction for 1972 is as follows:

Reconstructed balance sheet, 1972

$ Millions			
Cash and investments	10	Payables	20
Receivables	23	Subscriptions	15
Inventories	4		
Property, plant, etc.	60	Deferred tax	12
Goodwill	67	Long-term debt	32
		Shareholders' funds	85

Sources of capital

Goodwill was not being amortized as accounting rules did not require it at that time. Tangible assets other than machinery were minimal. Working capital was negative because of the benefit of advance subscriptions. There was a small net debt. WPC's business value could not be ascribed to its low asset base or its subscription income, although both of these were pluses. Its major source of economic goodwill was the importance of its products to readers, viewers, and advertisers. This was reflected in its record, its potential, and its ROE.

> **WPC's business value could not be ascribed to its low asset base or its subscription income, although both of these were pluses. Its major source of economic goodwill was the importance of its products to readers, viewers, and advertisers. This was reflected in its record, its potential, and its ROE.**

Return on equity

We can estimate the company's ROE from the reconstructed balance sheet and 1973's earnings. Two adjustments should be considered. First, goodwill. The bulk of this was likely to have been acquired with the TV stations and *Newsweek*. Without a series of balance sheets we cannot estimate IP and overcome the normal difficulties goodwill presents. A conservative assumption is to leave goodwill as stated. Since it has not been amortised no other adjustments are necessary. Second, tax. Apart from tax on its current earnings, WPC was also providing for deferred tax on its income statement. The notes to the accounts show that the deferred element largely related to subscription activities deducted as a cost when incurred for tax purposes but not shown on the income statement that year. When and if these costs reduced the deferred provision would become payable. In reality, as the subscription base was growing, these activities would continue at an increased level. If, in the distant future, tax related to 1973 activities had to be paid, inflation would render its real value immaterial. The cashflows confirmed that actual tax paid had not exceeded the current tax provision in recent years. Accordingly, it is reasonable to take a base net income that deducted current but not deferred tax. Our rough estimate of ROE is therefore:

$$ROE = \frac{\$16 \text{ million (1973 income net of current tax)}}{\$83 \text{ million (1972 shareholders' funds)}} = 19\%$$

What was WPC worth?

Based on this calculation the intrinsic value of WPC was:

$$\frac{\$16 \text{ million}}{(10\%)^2} \times 19\% = \$304 \text{ million}$$

If it is any consolation for the necessary roughness of this approach we know that in 1973 Buffett was not using the ROE method for this acquisition. It is in fact a rare example of his use of outside opinion to justify his estimate of value. It was an easy investment decision, he said – any banker, analyst, media broker or investor would have known that WPC was worth at least $400 million at this time. This is not a helpful statement for those not specializing in media valuation but he later explained it with some mathematics.

It was widely believed then that first-rate media businesses could increase their earnings at around 6 per cent p.a. forever without employing additional capital; this meant earnings equaled free cash-flow. The valuation of an infinite stream of earnings growing at a 6 per cent p.a. is solved by an undisputed formula:

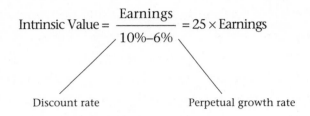

$$\text{Intrinsic Value} = \frac{\text{Earnings}}{10\%-6\%} = 25 \times \text{Earnings}$$

Discount rate   Perpetual growth rate

WPC's $16 million in earnings would by this calculation be worth $400 million.

WHAT BUFFETT DID

1973 was a bad year for the US stock markets. The average price fall was around 20 per cent and some sectors, including media, fell a lot further. Berkshire Hathaway used the opportunity to buy 467 150 "B" shares for $10.6 million, or $22.69 each. Taking into account both share classes and the considerable number of share options outstanding there were around 4.8 million common stock equivalents outstanding. Berkshire had, therefore, bagged around 10 per cent of the company at a price which valued the whole at $109 million. The margin of safety based on Buffett's published estimate of value was:

$$\text{Margin of safety} = \frac{\$400 \text{ million} - \$109 \text{ million}}{\$400 \text{ million}} = 73\%$$

At our lower estimate of $304 million, the margin was 64 per cent.

WHAT HAPPENED NEXT

Although Buffett has been influential at GEICO and has joined a number of boards of investee companies, WPC is probably where he has had most effect. He and Kay Graham became friends and he has also spent a lot of time with Graham's son, Don, who is now chairman and CEO. The first sign of his influence was when WPC started repurchasing its own stock, which it did in earnest from 1975.

Graham took on the unions in 1975. A four and a half month strike was settled with fresh union agreements. The newspaper continued to be published in a short form using other staff and printing plants. There was a temporary dent in advertising lineage, but hardly any effect on circulation: proof of the franchise. The rebound in 1976 profits was spectacular. Income after current taxes but before some goodwill amortization jumped to $28 million, 73 per cent ahead of 1973.

In the 25 years following Berkshire's investment, there have been acquisitions in the newspaper, magazine, and TV-station divisions. WPC also owns cables systems, an online information service and some other new businesses. Among large American media companies it has probably been the most disciplined in saying "no" to acquisitions and diversifications. Most of its free cash has paid down debt and repurchased shares. The *Washington Post* has gradually increased its circulation on weekdays and dramatically on Sundays. The cover price and advertising rates continue to rise, but in many ways little has changed.

Revenue for the company as a whole is still derived overwhelmingly from advertising and circulation. Since 1973 advertising revenue has grown 8 per cent p.a. and circulation revenue 10 per cent p.a. Pre-goodwill amortization, operating income has grown 12 per cent p.a., demonstrating improved margins, and net income 13 per cent p.a., because of the bias against debt. There are now almost 11 million common stock equivalents outstanding compared to 4.8 million in 1973, but the apparent increase is because of stock splits. While there has been some share issuance the equivalent number of shares has fallen heavily through stock repurchases and there are now over 40 per cent fewer shares outstanding than in 1973. Consequently, earnings per share have compounded at 16 per cent p.a.

Buffett and Munger have a more sanguine view of media businesses, especially newspapers, these days. They bought their own newspaper, the *Buffalo News* for $33 million in 1977; it made $33 million in 1997. While such businesses still have superior economics as low capital consumers and owners of loyal customers, the degree of their franchise has decreased. People watch more TV these days and this market has become more competitive. Accepting this, Buffett and Munger are loyal investors and have declared that they will never sell their stake in WPC.

WPC made $315 million net in 1997 and at the end of that year Berkshire's original $10.6 million was worth $841 million, a 19 per cent p.a. compound gain excluding dividends.

EXERCISES

1 Shareholders' equity was $1184 million at the end of 1997. What was IP over the whole period of the case? Is the answer interesting?

2 If the company had a six month strike in all of its businesses now, costing $100 million but creating no long-term problems, how would its value change?

Further questions for discussion

3 Buffett believes that newspaper economics have weakened in the past 20 years. Why do you think that is?

4 Where are the media monopolies of today?

18

Wells Fargo & Company

Berkshire Hathaway bought 5 000 000 ordinary stock of Wells Fargo & Company in 1989 and 1990 for $289.4 million. A further 1 791 218 shares were bought for $134.3 million in 1992 and 1993 and 500 200 were bought for $74.1 million in 1996:

Year	Shares purchased	Total number owned	Cost in year ($m)	Total cost ($m)	Cost per share ($)	Average cost per share ($)
1989–90	5 000 000	5 000 000	289.4	289.4	57.89	57.89
1991	0	5 000 000	0	289.4		57.89
1992	1 358 418	6 358 418	91.6	381.0	67.43	59.92
1993	432 800	6 791 218	42.7	423.7	98.66	62.39
1994	0	6 791 218	0	423.7		62.39
1995	0	6 791 218	0	423.7		62.39
1996	500 200	7 291 418	74.1	497.8	148.14	68.27

HISTORY

Wells Fargo is one of the most celebrated names in American commerce. Famous for its stagecoach operations in the 1850s, these were divested early in the twentieth century leaving a profitable bank based in San Francisco. There is an interesting link with another Berkshire investment since the founders, Henry Wells and William

Famous for its stagecoach operations in the 1850s, these were divested early in the twentieth century leaving a profitable bank based in San Francisco. There is an interesting link with another Berkshire investment since the founders, Henry Wells and William Fargo, had first worked together at the newly formed American Express.

Fargo, had first worked together at the newly formed American Express.

The American banking industry is predominantly regional in structure with a large number of banks, savings and loans, and credit unions by international standards. Like many of its peers, Wells Fargo grew by merging with and acquiring competitors in its home state, culminating with Crocker and Barclays California in the 1980s.

WELLS FARGO IN 1989 AND 1990

By 1989 the bank had come to be regarded as one of the best managed in the country. It had achieved that rare combination, a reputation for good and innovative service, and low costs. It had pioneered new and better retail delivery, with longer opening hours for its customers and led the way with more ATMs, telephone and online banking. At the same time, it had contained headcount so that its cost–income and return on asset ratios were among the best in the industry.

Return on Assets (ROA) = Net income/Average total assets.

By 1989 the bank had come to be regarded as one of the best managed in the country. It had achieved that rare combination, a reputation for good and innovative service, and low costs. It had pioneered new and better retail delivery, with longer opening hours for its customers and led the way with more ATMs, telephone and online banking.

In 1990, the Californian economy started to head toward recession. Southern California, in particular, had been hit by the "peace dividend". The rundown of the cold war had led to cutbacks in defence and aerospace spending, two of the region's largest industries. Although Wells Fargo's results did not yet reflect the consequences, it was vulnerable to an industrial or consumer slowdown or slump in its home state. The stock market promptly knocked 30–40 per cent off its market value.

Does the company provide value to its customers?

Wells Fargo had made several acquisitions but its organic growth was also good. By making it more convenient to bank it had attracted a larger share of the consumer market. It was offering more pension and equity-related savings products and, therefore, getting a higher share of its customers' savings. In the commercial loan arena, it had specialized in lending to large companies, into highly leveraged transactions and on property. It would come to regret some of this but overall it was able to benefit from concentrated expertise and low central costs.

Does the management provide value to the company?

Buffett believed that Carl Reichardt, chairman and CEO, and Paul Hazen, president and COO, were the best team in American banking. He said he was reminded of Tom Murphy and Dan Burke at Capital Cities – his all-time favorite managers. Clearly, they were able and worked well together. They also stuck to what they knew and did not diversify beyond their capacity to manage and understand. And in a recurring Buffettian theme they were committed to low costs in every aspect of their operation. Staffing is the largest single non-interest expense for most banks and keeping this cost low is important, but the expansion of non-traditional distribution channels, such as telephone banking, also allowed revenue to rise without

> Southern California, in particular, had been hit by the "peace dividend". The rundown of the cold war had lead to cutbacks in defence and aerospace spending, two of the region's largest industries.

increasing costs at traditional – and expensive – branches. In the six years from 1984 to 1989 while net interest income grew a compounded 15 per cent p.a. and non-interest income 24 per cent p.a., non-interest expense grew only 12 per cent p.a. In fact, cost management was even more important at Wells Fargo than it was at Capital Cities. TV stations had monopolistic qualities, but there are few such franchises in banking. Interest rates, loan policies, and most services are public and imitable. As at GEICO, the best protection from competition was sustained cost leadership.

Does the company provide value to its shareholders?

Banking is cyclical. Sometimes a bank's results follow the national or domestic economy's ups and downs. Equally often, they get into trouble all on their own. Wells Fargo had been pretty good at avoiding the potholes, generally by sticking to a few markets it knew well. There had been a big clearout of foreign exposure in 1987, but there had never been the same threat that lesser developed country debt had posed to the New York banks. This bank outperformed its peers on all key measures: its return on assets was high because of low costs and its ability to cross-sell a large number of fee-based businesses to its clients; and its return on equity was excellent. The danger that the stock market had sensed was real, however, as California's economy started to contract. The question was whether the market had overreacted.

> Wells Fargo had been pretty good at avoiding the potholes, generally by sticking to a few markets it knew well. There had been a big clearout of foreign exposure in 1987, but there had never been the same threat that lesser developed country debt had posed to the New York banks.

SOURCES OF INFORMATION

Buffett was a bank skeptic. Aside from the competitiveness of the market and their propensity for accidents banks were inherently risky. To understand why, you must split bank earnings into their three constituents. Banks make money by taking deposits at one price, lending the same money out at a higher price and charging fees for financial services. Although these are logically separate activities they are in practice entwined. A bank may not be able to attract depositors if it cannot at other times lend them money, and it will not be able to charge account fees if it does neither. (Some clever bankers can make money by just giving advice and providing other services but this is effectively a different industry with the same roots.) The difference between the price paid for deposits and the income charged for loans is a bank's net interest income and often forms the bulk of its

> Banks make money by taking deposits at one price, lending the same money out at a higher price and charging fees for financial services. Although these are logically separate activities they are in practice entwined.

earnings. An important aspect of this set-up is that deposits, which are chiefly personal savings, are borrowings under a different name. A typical bank will be borrowing between ten and twenty times' its shareholders' funds. Most depositors are insured by the government against loss and are, therefore, indifferent to the risks inherent in this arrangement. For the bank's shareholders it is a paying proposition because the bank is borrowing from its depositors at a lower rate than would otherwise be achievable. Nevertheless, there is a risk that something will go wrong. For example:

> A typical bank will be borrowing between ten and twenty times' its shareholders' funds. Most depositors are insured by the government against loss and are, therefore, indifferent to the risks inherent in this arrangement. For the bank's shareholders it is a paying proposition because the bank is borrowing from its depositors at a lower rate than would otherwise be achievable.

$ Millions	1996	1997
Loan assets	100	95
Deposits	95	95
Shareholders' equity	5	0

Only 5 per cent of this institution's loan assets have to become irrecoverable for it to become insolvent. Banks protect against this through careful underwriting and taking a spread of risks but, as we shall see, even the best managed company can face disaster after relatively small asset movements.

Berkshire Hathaway had made small investments in the sector before (and had even owned a bank outright until forced to divest by regulators) but there was little chance of fresh investment in any but the finest of the bunch.

QUESTIONS TO TEST YOUR UNDERSTANDING

Do you understand why people buy the product?

Banks were necessary to the economy but also something of a necessary evil. Bankers had had a poor reputation in the USA for over a century. They were castigated for tightness in recession and profligacy in booms. Large businesses and governments had overtaken banks in size and creditworthiness but they were still the central recyclers of funds for individuals and most businesses.

How would the industry change in the next ten years?

There was pressure from all sides. Even middle-sized companies could access the capital markets through commercial paper or privately placed bonds. Those who chose the familiarity and convenience of borrowing from banks could command fine rates. On the deposit side competitiveness was even deadlier. Money-market funds had come from nowhere to command some $500 billion of the savings market in a little over ten years. These were mutual funds benefiting from low operating costs and no insurance requirement. Finally, banking was still as competitive as any retail business and was faced with the challenge of adapting to new means of distribution – just as mail order, discount stores, and shopping malls had changed the agenda for all retailers.

Are you comfortable with the management?

If you were going to invest in this industry you needed to do so in partnership with managers who were able, honest and willing to stick to their knitting. Reichardt and Hazen passed these tests. The additional test for a competitive business was to operate at a low cost. Wells Fargo had made a habit of cutting expenses. Its cost–income ratio of 61 per cent and return on assets of 1.26 per cent in 1989 were at world-beating levels.

Are there substitutes?

Retail customers and small businesses are slow to move their principal banking relationship. Nonetheless a typical Californian individual or company had multiple alternative banks from which to choose plus the mutual cash funds and capital markets already mentioned.

FINANCIAL ANALYSIS

Balance sheets, 1988 and 1989

$ Billion			
Cash	2.9	Borrowings and deposits	43.2
Securities	1.7	Other	0.8
Loans	41.0	Subordinated debt	1.8
Other	3.1	Preferred stock	0.4
		Shareholder' equity	2.5

Wells Fargo's books looked sound. A simple measure of a bank's strength is its capital adequacy, comparing its capital to its assets, adjusted for the riskiness of those assets. The Federal Reserve Board's guidelines required 4 per cent of the risk-adjusted assets to be backed by shareholders' funds and 8 per cent by shareholders' funds plus some other long-term liabilities, including the subordinated debt and preferred stock shown in the table above. Wells Fargo's respective ratios were 5 per cent and 10 per cent, well above the minima. However, as we have seen, 5 or even 10 per cent of capital is little protection against loan losses; the $2.5 billion of ordinary capital would have been wiped out by a 6 per cent diminution of loan assets. How vulnerable was the bank to the anticipated Californian recession? Its loan portfolio broke down as follows:

$ Billion	1989	1988
Commercial	14.5	13.1
Real estate construction	4.1	4.4
First mortgage residential	7.6	5.1
Other real estate mortgage	6.0	5.5
Total real estate	13.6	10.6
Credit card	2.5	2.1
Other revolving credit	0.6	0.6
Monthly payment	1.3	1.4
Real estate junior residential	3.9	3.4
Total consumer	8.4	7.5
Lease financing	1.1	1.4
Foreign	0.1	0.6
Total	41.7	37.7

The $13.6 billion out of $41.7 billion (33 per cent) committed to real estate lending was not in itself worrying as many banks exceed this proportion; some *only* lend to this sector. The "real estate junior residential" category, that is, personal loans secured by second charge over a house should also be included, however. And included in "Commercial" was another $1.7 billion out to real estate developers. This takes the real estate share of total loans to 46 per cent. Perhaps more important was the share of real estate lending taken by construction loans (30 per cent). This was high compared to other commercial banks. Although the absolute amount appeared to fall between 1988 and 1989, this was actually accomplished by an accounting maneuver. Construction loans can be highly speculative and would have been the first and greatest casualties in a downturn.

> While one can see the high return on assets by comparing net income to the balance sheet assets, these figures do not reveal the potential volatility of one key figure. In regular times a bank's income statement will appear as above. But when times are either tough or booming "loan loss provision" comes into its own. This is a bank's own estimate of the losses it will ultimately suffer on its loans. What it actually receives or writes off is another question.

Income statements, 1988 and 1989

$ Millions	1989	1988
Interest income	4870	4178
Interest expense	(2712)	(2205)
Net interest income	2159	1972
Loan loss provision	(362)	(300)
Non-interest income	779	682
Non-interest expense	(1575)	(1519)
Income before tax	1001	835
Tax	(400)	(323)
Income after tax and preferred dividends	574	487

These numbers confirm how important net interest income is, even to a bank like this with plentiful fees and investment services income. While one can see the high return on assets by comparing net income to the balance sheet assets, these figures do not reveal the potential volatility of one key figure. In regular times a bank's income statement will appear as above. But when times are either tough or booming "loan loss provision" comes into its own. This is a bank's own estimate of the losses it will ultimately suffer on its loans. What it actually receives or writes off is another question. The provision is supposed to be a smoother measure of what will happen over a cycle. In practice most banks are either too optimistic or too pessimistic and this provision fluctuates widely. The 1988 and 1989 provisions of 0.8 per cent and 0.9 per cent of loans respectively were normal and respectable amounts. In 1987, though, the figure had been 2.4 per cent and the bank had barely broken even. The jump then had been the last element of dealing with lesser developed country problem loans and would not recur (foreign loans had virtually been extinguished from the portfolio). Problems could crop elsewhere, however. Some focused on highly leveraged transactions or leveraged buy-outs, which totaled $4.2 billion. The main worry was real estate.

Sources of capital

Banks were able to attract plentiful cheap-ish capital in the form of customers' deposits. Wells Fargo held $6.9 billion on which it paid no interest at all while the rest earned between 0 and 5 per cent below the rate at which banks lend to each other. Its average cost of funds was 5.7 per cent in 1989. Meanwhile, it was lending this money out at an average rate of 11.4 per cent. This was only a good idea to the extent that these loans continued to make money. Losses would depress the net return on assets and capital, but they could also destroy customer confidence and lead to a flight by depositors.

Return on equity

While 1.26 per cent was a high return on assets for a bank it would lead to extinction in almost any other industry. As ever, what we are more interested in is return on equity. A low ROA becomes a high ROE through leverage. Wells Fargo had 18 times as much debt as equity in 1989. Its ROE was as follows:

$$\text{ROE} = \frac{\$574 \text{ million (1989 net income after preferred dividends)}}{\$2315 \text{ million (1988–89 average common shareholders' funds)}} = 25\%$$

IP was slightly higher:

$$\text{IP} = \frac{\$574 \text{ million (1989 net income)} - \$487 \text{ million (1988 net income)}}{\$2456 \text{ million (1989 common equity)} - \$2174 \text{ million (1988 common equity)}} = 31\%$$

What was Wells Fargo worth?

Based on this calculation the Intrinsic Value of WPC was:

$$\frac{\$574 \text{ million}}{(10\%)^2} \times 31\% = \$17.8 \text{ billion}$$

using IP; or

$$\frac{\$574 \text{ million}}{(10\%)^2} \times 25\% = \$14.4 \text{ billion}$$

using ROE.

Most banks were not able to earn remotely near this ROE. An average bank, just like the average corporation, might expect to attain 10–12 per cent on its reinvested capital over time. This would justify an intrinsic value of some ten times earnings. However, investors in banks also faced big downside risks because of leverage.

Buffett wrote at the time of his initial purchases that Wells Fargo faced three specific risks. California might have an earthquake severe enough to devastate the local economy and bust banks, or general financial panic in the face of the oncoming business contraction could lead to a mass flight of depositors from every financial institution in the state, punishing good and bad banks alike. He thought neither of these possibilities likely. Finally, he recognized that Wells Fargo was a leading real estate lender and would be affected by a drop in land prices or demand. He looked at this risk coolly. The bank had earned $1 billion before tax in 1989 and $1.4 billion before tax and loan loss provisions. What if 10 per cent of all its loans ($4.2 billion) went bad? Each of these loans would have to lose 30 per cent of principal ($1.3 billion) to drive the company into loss. How likely was this? $4.2 billion would be 31 per cent of all real estate loans and unless the bank had been reckless in its lending or California went down the drain this was not a reasonable prediction. Equally, it is really quite difficult to lose 30 per cent of the principal of a portfolio of secured loans unless they are based on pure speculation. Wells Fargo had been an aggressive real estate lender but it did not have a reputation for being reckless or speculative. Buffett believed that even if the bank broke even one year, it could go back to earning a good ROE in more level times, just as it had after the developing country write-offs.

> Buffett wrote at the time of his initial purchases that Wells Fargo faced three specific risks. California might have an earthquake severe enough to devastate the local economy and bust banks, or general financial panic in the face of the oncoming business contraction could lead to a mass flight of depositors from every financial institution in the state, punishing good and bad banks alike. He thought neither of these possibilities likely.

WHAT BUFFETT DID

1990 was a terrible year for bank stocks; consequently an excellent year for buying banks. Wells Fargo continued to report solid quarterly results but other banks were starting to report losses and all stocks suffered. The curiosity was that Wells Fargo was cheap *even before* this happened. The $574 million net income earned in 1989 was equivalent to $11 per share. This outturn would have been highly predictable based on cumulative quarterly results throughout 1989. Yet the share price fluctuated only between $59 and $87, or a p/e of between 5.4 and 7.9. Berkshire bought at an average price of $58 in 1989 and 1990. Purchases were principally made in 1990 after the market became jittery. By this time results for 1990 were highly predictable, on the major assumption, explored above, that real estate-related loan loss provisions would be large but not solvency-threatening and subsequent provisioning would revert to mean. In 1990, compared to 1989, the bank had more assets, a higher book value and was reporting an even higher series of earnings. Again the full year result was predictable at $13.4 per share. The $58 average price paid therefore represented a p/e of 4.3. The total market capitalization at this price was $3 billion. Taking the more conservative 1989 earnings and the lower of the ROE and IP methods:

$$\text{Margin of safety} = \frac{\$14.4\ \text{billion} - \$3\ \text{billion}}{\$14.4\ \text{billion}} = 79\%$$

In summary, this was an institution where there was a low and calculable chance of losing everything. On the upside, if it survived and performed as an average bank, taking its intrinsic value to, say, ten times core earnings of c.$600–700 million or $6–7 billion, there was a good margin of safety of c.50 per cent. If, as expected, it was over time able to outperform its peers the margin of safety could be an excellent 79 per cent – each dollar invested could be expected to turn into five.

> **In summary, this was an institution where there was a low and calculable chance of losing everything.**

WHAT HAPPENED NEXT

$ Billions	1990	1991	1992	1993
Loans	47	43	36	32
Assets	54	52	51	51
Net interest income	2.3	2.5	2.7	2.7
Loan loss provision	(0.3)	(1.3)	(1.2)	(0.6)
Other income	0.9	0.9	1.1	1.1
Other expense	(1.7)	(2.0)	(2.0)	(2.2)
Net income	0.7	0	0.2	0.6
Shares outstanding	53	52	53	56
(Millions)				
EPS ($)	13.4	0	4.4	9.9
ROA (%)	1.4	0	0.5	1.2
ROE (%)	26.3	0	7.9	16.7

The feared southern Californian recession did come round the corner, wiping out companies and households. The effect was felt across the loan book, from credit-card delinquency to house repossession. As predicted, the worst casualties were real estate developers, who had built or were building properties they could not fill. Wells' figures also showed that large and leveraged companies, where the bank was also disproportionately exposed, were especially vulnerable. The magnitude of provisions required was higher than Buffett had predicted, probably by a factor of two. By the end of 1993, the total accrued and uncharged off provision for losses equaled 6.4 per cent of total loans; in 1990 it had been 1.8 per cent.

Yet, Berkshire added to its investment in 1992 and 1993, at a higher per-share price than it enjoyed in 1989 and 1990. Buffett could see, first and crucially, that the bank was not going bust. Although management properly added to its provisions in 1992 they were (a) affordable, (b) out of a higher income base, and (c) the last at this level that would be required. For beyond the horrid bottom line, the fundamentals for this business were actually improving. Regulatory capital ratios were now far stronger. The table shows that the total asset base shrank slightly but total loans within this fell dramatically. This was an immediate management response to the problems by reducing exposure to real estate development and the large company sector. The balance was temporarily invested in high-grade securities. Interest rates were fortuitously falling which helped recovery and the bond portfolio. Management planned to redeploy this capital gradually as recovery helped to expand small and medium-sized enterprises and consumers. Non-interest income grew, helped by management's long-standing commitment to increasing the customer base in low-cost ways (ATMs, branches in retailers, and electronic banking), higher charges levied on retail accounts, and good growth in retail securities business – the value of invested assets managed or advised by the bank now far exceeded the balance sheet assets. Equally important was the continuing expense control. Looking at the individual elements of overhead, what stands out is that salaries grew with inflation but all other items did not grow at all.

This all added up to the probability that Wells would be a far *more* profitable institution after the recession. An easy way to estimate this requires a view on loan losses. Excluding the "clear-out" years, loan loss provisions had rarely exceeded 0.7 per cent in any year. Applying this to the 1993 income statement, net income would have been c.$800 million (a similar result is derived from 1992 numbers). This would have given an ROE of some 23 per cent and hence an IV of $18.4 billion, or $330 per share. Berkshire's 1992–3 purchases at $67 and $99 were thus at a discount to value of 70–80 per cent. As so often is the case, even if you had been a Wells skeptic and afraid of its chances of survival, it would have been possible to buy at an attractive price long after the danger had passed. Even in conventional terms $99 was a 1993 p/e of only 10.

$ Billions	1994	1995	1996	1997
Loans	36	35	64	64
Assets	52	49	109	97
Net interest income	2.6	2.7	5.5	4.6
Loan loss provision	(0.2)	–	(0.1)	(0.6)
Other income	1.2	1.2	2.2	2.7
Other expense	(2.2)	(2.1)	(4.0)	(3.6)
Net income	0.8	1.0	1.7	2.0
Shares outstanding	54	49	83	89
(Millions)				
EPS ($)	14.8	20.0	20.0	21.9
ROA (%)	1.5	2.0	1.8	1.9
ROE (%)	22.5	24.9	15.1	14.5

The bottom line grew as expected in 1994 and 1995, aided by top line expansion, continuing cost control and low loan provisions. Earnings per share rose faster thanks to an aggressive new share repurchase scheme, which also took advantage of the continuing low stock price.

In early 1996 Wells bought a Californian bank of almost the same size, First Interstate, in an all-share swap valued at c.$11 billion. The chance to consolidate in California, primarily through branch mergers and closures, was somewhat muffed by Wells' management. The projected $800 million p.a. cost savings were not quite reached. More worryingly there was a series of computer and human errors leading to mistakes such as "misplaced deposits". Competitors took advantage of these errors and the branch rationalizations and soon the merged bank was losing customers. There are recent signs that this customer loss has been stabilized.

> Regardless of this recent stumble, Wells Fargo's stock price has had an excellent run-up since the dark days of 1990–92.

Regardless of this recent stumble, Wells Fargo's stock price has had an excellent run-up since the dark days of 1990–92. At year-end 1997, the per share price was $339, compared with Berkshire's average cost of

$68 and, excluding dividends, the compound annual capital gain is c.28 per cent.

Berkshire trimmed a number of its shareholdings in 1997, including the sale of 8 per cent of its Wells Fargo shares. This 8 per cent reduction recovered more than 40 per cent of the total cost of its stake.

EXERCISES

1 If depositors had lost confidence at the end of 1989 the bank might have had to increase its capital base. Say it had raised $500 million at $58 per new share. What would the effect have been on intrinsic value?

2 Were you an existing shareholder in this scenario, what would you have lost?

Further questions for discussion

3 Why is a loss in depositor confidence so serious for a bank? Why hasn't government insurance protecting loss to depositors mitigated this risk?

4 Calculate ROA and ROE for your own bank.

ANSWERS TO EXERCISES

Chapter 12: American Express

1 The check float was $4.8 billion. If this liability no longer existed, share-holders' equity would have had to increase by this amount to $11.1 billion.

2 Continuing net income of $1.2 billion is unaffected so ROE is

$$\frac{1.2}{11.1} = 10.8\%$$

3
$$\$1.2 \text{ billion} \times \frac{10.8}{(10\%)^2} = \$13 \text{ billion}$$

4 Since the market capitalization in 1994 was c.$15.7 billion it is unlikely that one would have made further commitments.

Chapter 13: Coca-Cola

1

$ Billions	Net income	Shareholders' equity	Return on average equity
1985	943	5958	
1986	1149	7030	17.7
1987	1336	6448	19.8

2 IP in 1985–86 is about the same as the 1987 ROE. Intrinsic Value might be

$$\$1336 \text{ million} \times \frac{19.8\%}{(10\%)^2} = \$26 \text{ billion}$$

3 Including the bottling activity clearly (and definitionally) reduced ROE. The estimated intrinsic value of $26 billion is equivalent to a p/e of 19.8. Coca-Cola traded at a p/e of c.17 in early 1988, a shallow margin of safety. To produce a 50 per cent margin of safety the share price would have had to drop by some 40 per cent.

Chapter 14: GEICO

1 The most straightforward answer is that the lower the ratio the higher the profit, for a given level of premiums.

2 A low combined ratio means that an insurer can continue to write business that would be unprofitable to its competitors. This is a particular strength in a cyclical industry like insurance. When premium income has fallen or losses are temporarily high the low ratio company can continue to write business, both adding to its profits and gaining market share.

3 As we saw in the case a combined ratio below 100 implies that the float comes free. This means that the company rarely needs to consume capital, a very rare advantage in commerce.

Chapter 15: Gillette

1 Accounting decisions do not affect intrinsic value because they do not affect cash. Gillette would be no more or less valuable if it changed this policy. The practical effect would be to increase both income and shareholders' equity, so there would also be no change to IP.

2 A real cash saving of 5 per cent of sales would have added $179 million to pre-tax income in 1988 or c.$107 million at the prevailing tax rate to give net income of $376 million. We used an IP of 24 per cent in the case. An increase in net income of 40 per cent would pro rata to an IP of 34 per cent.

Chapter 16: Walt Disney

1 $4 million bought 5 per cent so the whole company was (market) valued at $80 million in 1966. In 1995 there were 525 million shares trading at $58 each; this equals $30.5 billion market capitalization. This equates to an annual compound return of c.22 per cent. This is an excellent return but the investment in Berkshire has actually produced a far greater profit.

2 A 22 per cent p.a. return over seventy-two years is 1 651 611 times the original investment. Dividing this into the $30.5 billion achieved gives a starting point of $18 467. In practice dividends will affect this result materially.

Chapter 17: Washington Post

1 The long term IP is

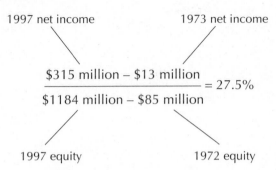

1997 net income   1973 net income

$$\frac{\$315 \text{ million} - \$13 \text{ million}}{\$1184 \text{ million} - \$85 \text{ million}} = 27.5\%$$

1997 equity   1972 equity

The answer is not interesting because the 1972 figures are too small to make any difference – this is really a measure of current ROE. IP works best over a small number of years.

2 Buffett has likened these short-term problems to posting a dividend that gets lost: the shareholder loses the dividend but the value of the company is otherwise unchanged. Therefore, in this case the value of the company would reduce by $100 million.

Chapter 18: Wells Fargo

1 Return on average equity was 25 per cent. The key assumption is that Wells Fargo could have made the same proportionate return to the new equity. If so, then $500 million would have produced incremental income of $125 million and total 1989 net income of $699 million. Logically applying the same ROE would have brought intrinsic value to $17.5 billion.

2 The existing market capitalization was c.$3.1 billion (53 million shares outstanding at $58 per share). Raising $500 million would have meant selling 16.3 per cent of the enlarged company. The intrinsic value of this stake was some $2.8 billion (16.3 per cent of $17.5 billion). Existing shareholders would have effectively been giving away $2.3 billion, the difference between cost and value.

Index